Search For The Grail

A Man's Guide For Developing An Inner Life

Ken Schmitz

The picture on the cover of the book is of Montsegur, a 13th century Cathar Castle located in the south of France. Some legends name Montsegur as the mythical Grail Castle. Something is inviting and summoning about a castle high on a hill. Something in one's soul wants to reach for it—this is the soul's yearning for wholeness."

ISBN : 1-4196-3919-6

To order additional copies, please contact us.
BookSurge, LLC
www.booksurge.com
1-866-308-6235
orders@booksurge.com

Search For The Grail

Search For The Grail

This book is dedicated to all who seek to live life with soul.

Acknowledgments

Jungian analyst Robert Johnson first taught me the value of an inner life. As a young man, I read everything he had written and in the 1980's I attended as many of his public lectures as I could. I consider Robert Johnson's influence on me to be one of the great blessings of my life. I value not only his teaching and writing, but also the rich, although brief, conversations we have had over the years.

Tom Lavin, a Jungian analyst in Chicago, has heard and discussed with me hundreds of my dreams. With his guidance I have deepened my commitment to my inner life and discovered parts of myself I did not know. The impetus and energy for this book is a direct result of my own dream work. I greatly appreciate Tom's gentle wisdom, love of the soul, and ability to laugh at life's twists and turns.

This book evolved from a course that I have presented to men over the past several years. More than fifty men have participated in this program. I have been inspired by their persistence and courage as they faced their wounds and shared their soul-journey with each other. In addition, they showed me that men are hungry for a myth that can speak to their life's struggles. I am especially grateful to the men who shared their dreams as examples for this book. I hope their work will inspire you as you read their accounts and see what ordinary men can do when they honor their inner life.

I would like to express my gratitude to the people who have read the draft of this book and shared their helpful comments. Kathryn Harwig saw this book in me before I did. Besides her editorial comments, her encouragement helped me undertake this project. John Curran, M.D., a colleague and a wonderful friend, has read the Grail story in its original 400 pages and he has discussed it with me for years. I have incorporated his valuable comments and suggestions into this book. Ed Sellner, a friend for more than forty years, not only shared his expertise as an author, but also invited me to present these ideas to the men's spirituality group at his college.

Sheila McCarry generously helped to edit and ready this manuscript for printing. I appreciate her kindness, her attention to detail, and her fierceness in tackling this task.

Finally, Judy Jackson, my wife, has been my biggest supporter during the writing of this book. She is the visionary in our relationship and she helped me see the Grail as the vessel in a committed relationship through which consciousness is trying to emerge. More important, in our marriage she holds my feet to the fire of transformation. Judy has challenged me to see the difference between the conscious feminine and the mother complex. Her wisdom and vitality are an invisible presence throughout this text. I am thankful to Life for giving me Judy, the companion my soul needed.

Preface

The soul of this book is the story of Parzival's search for the Grail. This beautiful legend is a metaphor and a roadmap for the psycho-spiritual development of a human being. Joseph Campbell suggests that the Grail is the symbol of the highest spiritual achievement in the Western world. To find the Grail is to know and live the full human and spiritual meaning of one's life. The premise of this book is that the Grail is within every human heart and that learning to form a loving and conscious relationship with one's inner world is the way to the Grail.

Of the many versions of the Grail quest, I have chosen *Parzival* by Wolfram von Eschenbach, because it speaks most directly to me. It is my story. I spent thirteen years as a member of a Catholic monastic community before leaving the priesthood to live as a married man. Parzival's story speaks to me of the joys and pains of living my own unique journey. Over the years I have seen many men discover the parallel between their life's journey and this story. I hope as you read this book that you, too, will discover important aspects of your life in this tale. *Parzival* is a wonderful story, filled with much wisdom and guidance. However, reading more than 400 pages of medieval English can be an overwhelming task for many of us today with the time constraints of work and family obligations. Yet I know this tale has much relevancy for us today. Therefore, I have decided to tell this tale wherever I can. I have told it publicly to hundreds of people over the years. I hope you come to love this magnificent story as much as I do.

The reader can approach this text in several ways. Each chapter contains three segments: practical guidance for creating and maintaining a relationship with your inner world, a segment of the Parzival myth and commentary on how it applies to a man's life, and journal questions to help you apply the themes of the story to your own life. I suggest that you answer the journal questions at the end of each chapter before going on to the next section. In this way you will be taking your own journey along with Parzival. Since this material is usually presented in a group with discussion and responses, I think that having one or several trusted friends who are reading and discussing the material with you would be very helpful. On the other hand some of you may want to read it cover to cover, or focus mainly on the story, or on the inner work sections. This format provides several options for the reader.

At the back of the book I have added a list of characters with a brief description of each character, so that you can keep track of the names as the story unfolds.

The ideas presented in this book focus primarily on a male perspective, because the story is rich with issues and processes that are unique to men. We live in a culture where so many men have not been initiated into a healthy, mature, and a creative masculinity. Without elders to guide and model maturity, many men are left performing prescribed societal roles and they bear the confusion, anger, and discontent of living a life that is not really authentically their own. When a man lives a life that is opposing his true nature, something within him rebels and seeks its own expression. However, without guidance from men who have previously walked their own path and discovered a way to live a soul-filled life, the likelihood of becoming lost greatly increases. The legend of Parzival can serve as a guide for the man seeking an alternative to living a prescribed life.

I believe women can also benefit from this material. Many issues that Parzival faces are universal and therefore will speak to women as well. By reading this book, women may come to understand the complexity and depth of the men in their lives. Healthy relationships with women play an important role in a man's ability to know himself. Therefore, a woman who knows and understands a man's struggles can be a significant partner in his search for his soul. Likewise, a man who is willing to learn about a woman's unique journey is a valuable partner for her maturing. This myth can also be helpful in a woman's individual journey as she struggles to develop a strong, mature, masculine side of her personality. To explore this topic in greater detail, I refer the reader to the work of Marion Woodman.[1]

The Parzival tale addresses life from the point of view of a heterosexual man. However, I have found that many principles and dynamics of the story apply directly to gay men and to their partners whom I have known and counseled over the years. At its most basic level, Parzival's search for the Grail is a story about how to be an authentic and embodied human being despite the many factors that make each life unique.

In writing this book I have gathered and summarized material from three main sources and arranged it so that it is accessible to the lay person. My introduction to the Parzival myth came through the work of Joseph Campbell. In *The Power of Myth* and in *Transformations of Myth through Time*, Campbell gives an extensive background to the Grail myths and especially to Wolfram's version, *Parzival*. Campbell's insights and perspective have guided me in the writing of this book.

The second major influence in this book is the work of the spiritual teacher Rudolf Steiner. About ten years ago my wife and I were on the faculty of a retreat for spiritual seekers. We were presenting material on the Grail myth as it relates to couples. We had the good fortune of meeting another faculty member Robert Sardello whose lecture complemented our presentation. During one of our informal conversations, he recommended the book *The Ninth Century* by Walter J. Stein. In this book Stein discusses the Parzival myth in light of the teachings of Rudolf Steiner. I have found Steiner's insights into the spiritual evolution of consciousness to be very helpful in my understanding of the Parzival tale.

Another significant resource in the development of this text is Robert Johnson's book *He* in which he tells the French version of the Parzival story. The German version, which I am using, borrows heavily from the French version in the early parts of the tale. Johnson's commentaries about the young Parzival, especially his insights into the "Fool's Clothing" and "Red Knight" aspects of a man's personality, have shaped my understanding of the psychological significance of the myth. In the sections on the inner life, I present the models for dream work and active imagination contained in Johnson's book *Inner Work*.

Finally, my personal experience of the reality of the inner world has guided me to write this book. Robert Johnson taught me the value of developing a relationship with my inner world of dreams, thoughts, and emotions. One day in the mid-1980's I was attending a week-long conference in North Carolina where Robert Johnson was part of the faculty. I was taking an afternoon walk through the woods, pondering my dream from the previous night, when Robert came walking on another path that joined mine. He asked if he could walk with me. As we talked about the conference and what I was learning, I asked if I could tell him my dream from the night before. He listened with interest. In the dream I saw a beautiful tree against the Eastern sky. In the tree I saw a mandala (circle) with a design that was only half finished. Johnson talked to me about the symbolism of the dream. Because of his understanding of the design in the mandala, he told me that the dream was emphasizing the importance of the feminine in our world. He felt that I would be making a contribution in this area. However, he cautioned me to make the clear distinction between the "feminine" and the "mother complex." I have attempted to fulfill that task in this book. Twenty years later, I am still working with the message of that dream, and Johnson's words regarding the feminine still challenge me.

Men misunderstand and often sarcastically degrade the feminine side of their psyche in everyday conversations with each other. Although criticizing something we do not understand or are afraid of is understandable, mockery of the feminine side of men is harmful. I believe that men today are evolving and creating a fuller understanding of what it means to be male. We are discovering that a developed feminine side is necessary for healthy living. Developing the feminine side of a man's psyche does not make him unmanly. Instead, his instincts, his emotions, the wisdom contained in his body through his gut feeling, and the value of being relational inform and enrich his life. A man does not develop his feminine side to diminish the strength of his masculine nature, but as a necessary complement for a healthy, loving, and balanced personality. The story of Parzival and the process of developing an inner life through dream work, which are the focus of this book, emphasize the value of the feminine side of the male psyche.

For many generations our culture has socialized men to be one-sided, rigidly strong, stoic, and in-charge. Relationships and marriages in the twenty-first century will no longer tolerate a man who continues to maintain a power-over stance with his partner and with his own psyche. In this book I will discuss practical ways for men to come to know and integrate the unknown, under-developed, and unexpressed sides of their personality.

The story of Parzival can give guidance to men who are seeking to overcome their one-sided way of living that results in broken relationships and self-alienation. In addition, developing the knowledge of the inner world and the skill of working with our dreams can provide a rich source of creative energy and hope for men who want to live a full, human life.

Easter 2006

Introduction

Sigune

The Grieving Human Soul

Life is a significant struggle for many of us in the Western culture.
Although we enjoy economic advantages far beyond those of previous
generations, a deep hunger for meaning permeates our society. A life
without meaning is a life disconnected from soul—disconnected from
our truest nature.

By soul I mean the part within each of us that is our authentic
and truest self. To live from our soul is to live as we were created to be.
However, soulful living has become difficult to achieve in our culture.
The social and religious institutions that once held meaning are no
longer effective in calling forth, nourishing, and enhancing soul for
many of us. Therefore, people struggle to make a heartfelt connection
to their own souls. Without a connection to soul, life becomes routine,
empty, and often self-destructive—life is a Waste Land.

The problem of the Waste Land is the major issue that all of
the Grail myths address. In every version of the tale, the Grail King
is wounded. When the King is wounded, the entire kingdom suffers.
The people are in sorrow. The land does not produce fruit or crops.
Emptiness and toil abound. Joy is absent. The medieval Waste Land is a
metaphor for the struggle of meaninglessness in our current time. One
could describe today's Waste Land as a life filled with anxiety, conflict,
and addictive behaviors that seek to fill a hole with experiences that
ultimately leave us more empty. When we are in the Waste Land,
life consists of tedious work that has no personal meaning. We also
experience the Waste Land when we are in broken relationships with
conflicts that we are unable to resolve. To live in such a Waste Land is
to suffer a wound of the soul.

For many years now the myths concerning the Grail and the Quest have moved me. Wolfram's Grail legend, *Parzival*, tells the story of a man's search for his true nature and his authentic life. Wolfram's tale gives direction and insight into how the Waste Land can be healed. I believe that its powerful message is still relevant and urgently needed today.

At this point one might ask why use a myth to address the problem of meaninglessness and inauthentic lives. What does a myth written more than 800 years ago have to say to twenty-first century life? I once heard Robert Bly say that birds contain their instinctive wisdom in their brains. How else would they know where to fly each season, where to return, and how to build their specific kind of nest? He also said that human beings store their wisdom in their myths.[1] Myths, which contain universal meaning, are stories told from generation to generation. They provide doorways to personal knowledge and wisdom for a society. Myths are to a society as dreams are to an individual. Just as a dream is a pictorial representation of what is taking place in the individual psyche, a myth is a pictorial representation of what is taking place in the collective psyche of the culture. Wolfram's Grail myth addresses the problem of the Waste Land today and contains the wisdom for healing the pain of meaningless lives. The re-emergence of the image of the Grail in popular culture is no accident. The wisdom, truth, and guidance contained in this twelfth century myth are desperately needed today, because we are living in a confusing and fearful time that lacks social, political, and religious leaders who can wisely guide us.

One unique aspect of the Grail stories is their emphasis on each person's unique search for meaning, instead of merely accepting society's prescribed definition of a meaningful life. An important scene occurs in one version of the Grail myth. The knights are sitting with Arthur before a meal and suddenly the Grail, covered by a veil, appears hovering over the table. Such a vision deeply moves the knights. The Grail then disappears. Gawain, Arthur's nephew, stands up and proposes an adventure for the court. He implores each knight to seek the Grail unveiled, since that day they had experienced it covered. The knights take up the challenge and begin to search the forest for the Grail. Each follows his own path where no man has traveled. In fact, it was considered a disgrace for any man to take the path already carved by another. If he did, it would go badly for him.[2] Anyone who searches for the Grail—for the authentic life in these modern times, must seek and find his or her own unique and individual path. Other people's experiences and wisdom can be very helpful in guiding us, but we must apply this help to our own unique life. No one can do it for us. Others can support, encourage, and guide, but it is ultimately a solo journey. Though we have to travel life in our unique way, we have tremendous aid and resources for the journey coming not only from others, but also most significantly from within ourselves.

Such an inner resource appears in the Parzival story as a woman named **Sigune**. She represents Parzival's soul. When Parzival first meets her, she is holding on her lap her beloved, a knight who has been killed. Sigune is weeping uncontrollably for him. This image is the picture from the soul's point of view of what it is like when a person is disconnected from his or her true nature, that is, from his or her own soul. The soul grieves because the person, her beloved, is dead to her.[3] We meet Sigune at four key moments in Parzival's journey. Each time we see that her demeanor changes as a reflection of Parzival's relationship to his own soul.

I find it a comforting and profound idea that within each of us lives a Sigune, our soul, who suffers incredible pain because of our separation from her. When we are dead to her, that is, when we are in our own Waste Land, she mourns for us. She does not leave us. She suffers the grief. Holding her beloved, she mourns the separation. As we will see throughout the story, Sigune will help Parzival eventually discover his true purpose in life. To learn to relate lovingly to one's soul is to find the Grail; to live from one's soul is to heal the Waste Land. The story of Parzival shows us what will heal the Waste Land within us and in our culture.

Let us now begin our journey, step by step, with Parzival's story as our road map. The situations and experiences he encounters are the same issues we must face as we search for our Grail, for that which gives our life personal and spiritual meaning. We will begin by taking a closer look at the Grail, the ultimate object of Parzival's search.

Chapter One

The Father

Background to the Grail

No other myth in Western literature touches the human imagination like the quest for the Grail. Most Westerners instantly recognize the idea of the Grail Quest, though few of us have actually read the story. One day I was preparing the conference room for one of my men's groups. In the center of the table I had placed a large stone bowl on a green cloth and on either side of the bowl a candle—one black and one white. It so happened that a man in his thirties, who looked as though he might be interested in motorcycles or NASCAR, walked by the room. He poked his head in and said, "Say, what is all this for?" I told him briefly about the group and that we use the legend of the Grail as a story for developing an inner life. He said with a grin, "Oh, my God, I have been looking for the Grail all my life and it is right here in this conference room." I had a good laugh with him and said, "Who would have thought about looking for it here, in a basement conference room?" He walked away laughing. However, the image of the Grail had touched him and he instantly recognized something—something came alive in him. Symbols that point to universal truths resonate in our hearts and minds. The Grail is such a symbol.

We have many different accounts of the Grail legend. In all versions the Grail is a vessel that dispenses whatever the seeker needs to give his or her life its ultimate meaning. The Grail contains inexhaustible vitality that can heal the wounded King and the Waste Land. However, the Grail itself does not automatically heal the wounded King. The King is healed when a knight with a noble and compassionate heart comes to the Grail Castle and, upon seeing the suffering King and the Grail, asks the correct question. Only then can the healing occur. Finding the Grail is only part of the journey. Asking the correct question with compassion releases the healing properties of the Grail.

The Grail is in each human heart. The inner world is the focus of our search and asking the right questions is essential for releasing the blessings of the Grail. Then, and only then, can we heal our own wounded King and transform our personal Waste Land. Because the questions are essential, a series of questions will follow each segment of the Parzival story. When we intentionally and consciously ask ourselves a question, the unconscious with its deep wisdom has something to respond to. Even if we do not know the answer to a question, writing it down in a journal and taking it seriously activate the inner world, and our unique answer to the question will begin to unfold. Serious questions take time to answer and the answers change as we progress though our life. During our journey we may entertain some of the following questions. Is there more to life than this? Why am I so discouraged and uninspired? Am I living someone else's idea of my life? What issues that are essential to my well-being am I not addressing? What is my role in the conflict with my spouse or my children? Why do things not work out well for me? What do I really value in my life? Asking the questions and living with them are essential elements of the quest. All versions of the Grail search invite a discussion about life questions, but Wolfram's version of the Grail legend takes the reader in a unique and profoundly important direction.

Wolfram offers a unique perspective to his Grail story. Unlike most of the other authors of the Grail legends, Wolfram was a knight. His experience as a knight allows him to describe the battlefields of medieval Europe in vivid detail. In describing Parzival's early years, Wolfram borrows heavily from the French version, *Percevel* written by Chrétien de Troyes. However, Wolfram's story has a completely different geographic and philosophic landscape than all other Grail stories. In Wolfram's version Parzival's journey to the Grail Castle is unique, as are many characters, including his wife. The origin of the Grail itself, the Grail King's wound, and the way the healing question is formed are all distinctive to Wolfram's version and reveal his unique philosophy.

Wolfram reveals his view of humankind in the first paragraph of the story. There he presents us with the image of the magpie, a bird with an equal amount of black feathers and white feathers. Wolfram compares every person with the magpie when he says, "for both colors have a share in him, the color of heaven and the color of hell."[1] It is a psychological truth that we have a dual nature within us. For every ounce of love a person has, he or she also has an equal amount of selfishness. For every ounce of hope one has, there exists an equal amount of despair. For every ounce of honesty one has, there exists an equal amount of dishonesty.

Having these unsavory qualities does not make a person good or bad. The human psyche is constructed in this way. What we do with these contradictory energies and the choices that we make determine our ethical and moral character. By using the image of the magpie, Wolfram is saying that these seemingly opposing qualities live within each of us. He is challenging us to ask ourselves how we are going to deal with these contradicting psychic forces. What we do with the black feathers and white feathers within us will determine how possible it is for us to understand our nature fully and to reach our own Grail. Wolfram gives us a clue about how to deal with these forces by the name that he gives the hero of the story. He tells us that Parzival means "the one who pierces the valley." Parzival will learn how to pierce through the middle of his opposing psychic forces. Parzival is the one who knows how to operate between the black feathers and the white feathers of his nature. Wolfram is urging the reader to become a Parzival. To become a Parzival is a significant first step toward discovering our Grail.

The Grail takes many forms in the various accounts of the tale. In the early Celtic versions the Grail is a vessel, a cornucopia dispensing the fruits of life. In Chrétien's version the Grail is a chalice. The ecclesiastical versions depict the Grail as the chalice that Jesus used at the Last Supper. Wolfram's Grail is a stone vessel from heaven. In this image we again see the opposites: stone, a common earth element, that comes from heaven. Wolfram tells us that the neutral angels brought the Grail to earth. By using this description of the Grail's origin, Wolfram is referring to an earlier creation myth, the battle of heaven. After God created the earth and especially His prize creation, the human being, He ordered His angels to bow to man. Lucifer refused and a battle resulted until God's angels expelled him from heaven. According to the creation myth, some angels chose God's side, while other angels chose Lucifer's side. However, according to Wolfram some angels chose neither side. These neutral angels, who held the ground between the white angels and the dark angels, brought the Grail to the earth and they are its guardians.

Wolfram's image of the magpie and his description of the neutral angels reveal his radical philosophy. He is making the clear distinction between perfection and wholeness. Our Judeo-Christian culture admonishes us to be perfect and to rid ourselves of evil. It is as if that instruction tells us that being human is wrong. Deep within ourselves we know that we cannot be gods; we know that we are not perfect and cannot be. We fail before we begin and we often judge ourselves negatively because we are not perfect. Therefore, shame is our inheritance. However, wholeness, that is, accepting that we have both black feathers and white feathers, is something we can achieve. Wholeness and healing do not tend toward perfection; they tend toward completeness. Wolfram advises us to be a Parzival, to pierce through the middle of the opposites in our psyche. If we can consciously hold both sides of our nature—the light side and the dark side—a new self will emerge and we will become more authentic. If we relinquish the illusion that we can create something perfect in the human realm, we have a chance to become a Parzival.

The Grail represents the unending source of life within us. How we can learn to experience this life force is the focus of this book. We will use the story of Parzival as our guide. The first step on his journey is to come to terms with his relationship to his father. A father plays a crucial role in helping his son develop into an emotionally and spiritually healthy man. When a father is absent, like Parzival's father, a boy struggles to find his identity. Many men in this culture miss a deep connection with their fathers. As a result they reflect this absence by lives that are confused, lonely, or dependent on others to affirm them. As we meet Parzival's father, begin to think of your relationship with your father.

The Story and Commentary

Parzival's story begins long before he was born—it begins with the lives of his family. His father is the great warrior **Gahmuret.** When the story opens, Gahmuret's father has just died. The custom of the land dictated that Gahmuret's older brother inherits all of the father's land in France. However, his brother being an unusually kind person, offers to share the kingdom equally with Gahmuret.

Gahmuret is an adventurer and a warrior by nature. As often happens, a new phase of a man's life begins upon the death of his father. Gahmuret politely refuses his brother's generous offer and states his desire to serve the mightiest man on the earth. It makes no difference to Gahmuret whether the man he chooses to serve is Christian or heathen, only that he is the mightiest. This was a bold and shocking statement for the thirteenth century reader, because most of Europe was engaged in the Crusades, fighting to recapture the Holy Land from the Moslems. Nevertheless, Gahmuret is an exceptional man who follows his own inner guidance that sometimes opposes the commonly acceptable way.

Having heard of the mighty Caliph of Baghdad, Gahmuret is determined to serve him. After a tender goodbye to his brother and to his mother, Gahmuret departs with his troops on his adventure to the Middle East. There he offers himself to the service of the Caliph of Baghdad and serves him bravely, and in so doing he develops a reputation as a great warrior.

Gahmuret's adventures eventually take him to Northern Africa, where he comes upon a castle that is under siege by two armies. To the west is an army of black men and to the east is an army of white men from Europe. The castle belongs to a black queen named **Belacane.** Gahmuret rides into the city filled with many wounded men and horses. Belacane greets him and tells him her predicament. She loves her city and her people and fears for their destruction. She begs for Gahmuret's assistance. Moved by her story and her tender heart, Gahmuret offers himself into her service. The next morning Gahmuret faces the leaders of the white army and defeats them in several jousting matches. They yield to him and pledge to end their siege of the castle. In the afternoon he defeats the leaders of the black army. The bravery and heroism of Gahmuret fill Belacane with deep gratitude and affection for him.

She knows she has found her man. Gahmuret is also very attracted to Belacane. They marry and soon after she conceives a child. Belacane gives birth to a son who has unusual markings. His skin and his hair are black and white, like the magpie. They name him **Feirefiz**. Wolfram tells us that he will grow up to be a strong warrior. He calls Feirefiz a "waster of forests" because, with his strength and knightly skill, he will shatter many spears and he will puncture many shields.

Unfortunately for Belacane and Feirefiz, Gahmuret has combat and adventure in his blood. Settling to be king of Belacane's land is not enough for him—he is restless. Although Gahmuret's strength is his bravery, his weakness is his inability to be faithful to a woman. One night he writes Belacane a goodbye letter and secretly leaves her for more adventure. In the letter he gives her the excuse that were she a Christian he might have stayed. This is an example of a typical male problem. Many men can perform incredible acts of strength and endurance in their work life, but their courage fails them when challenged to face the woman in their life honestly.

Belacane is heartbroken when she reads Gahmuret's letter. She knows that if he had told her that becoming Christian would have kept him with her, she would have gladly obliged. She is overwrought with sorrow. Belacane comforts herself by kissing the various spots on her darling son Feirefiz. She especially kisses his white spots, for they remind her of Gahmuret's blood flowing in his veins. Sadly, she is left to raise this boy alone without a father.

Gahmuret has gone back to Europe seeking more adventure. He comes upon a jousting tournament. Many knights from throughout Europe have assembled for this match. The prize for the winner will be the hand of the beautiful queen **Herzeloyde**. She is a widow whose husband died in battle. Gahmuret wins the tournament and the hand of the queen. Instantly she falls in love with him. They marry and soon she conceives a son.

As we have seen before, Gahmuret has competitiveness and adventure in his blood. Before long he wants to return to the Middle East and continue his service to the Caliph of Baghdad. Gahmuret is learning. Instead of secretly leaving, this time he tells Herzeloyde of his intentions. However, he knows that no matter what she says, he will leave anyway. Gahmuret, who continues to show his inability to be faithful to a woman (this time a baptized one), leaves his wife who is pregnant with Parzival. As often happens, a father's weakness becomes the issue with which a son must wrestle. Parzival too will need to learn how to become faithful to a woman.

One day, only two weeks before Parzival's birth, Herzeloyde is taking a midday nap and she has a horrific, precognitive dream:

> ...she thought a falling star was sweeping her into the air where fiery thunderbolts struck upon her with violence. These flew at her all at one time, and then her braids crackled and sang with sparks. With a crashthe thunder made its rush in a gust of burning tears. As she came to consciousness, there a griffon wrenched her right hand away. Then allwas changed. She imagined fantastic things—how she was nurse to a dragon that tore her womb, and how this dragon took suck at her breasts, and how he swiftly fled away and left her so that she never saw him again. Her heart was bursting out of her body and yet could not help but see that thing of terror. Seldom has anguish the like of that befallen a woman in her slumber. Previous to this she had been radiantly fair, but alas! how all that is changed: now she became sorrow's color. Long and broad her grief became, and future affliction drew near her.[2]

Upon awakening, Herzeloyde's servants comfort her, but they cannot quiet her inner knowing. Soon after, one of Gahmuret's squires enters her room to deliver the terrible news: the great Gahmuret died on the battlefield. The squire describes his burial in the fields of the Middle East. The Moslems so respected and loved Gahmuret that on his grave they placed a cross next to his helmet. Part of the inscription on the grave read: "He was baptized and supported the Christian law, but his death was a grief to the Moslems."[3] Gahmuret had accomplished a remarkable feat for his times. He lived with honor and integrity in both the Christian and the Moslem worlds. The ability to hold within himself these opposites, as we will see, will be a great asset to both of his sons. The themes in this myth are especially relevant today as our world struggles to live in harmony with the Christian and Moslem points of view.

The death of Gahmuret devastates Herzeloyde. If it were not for our hero Parzival moving in her womb, she may not have had the will to live. What a start to our story! We have two widows: a black queen in the east and a white queen in the west. We also have two fatherless boys: Feirefiz, the black-and white-skinned boy and the soon-to-be-born fair skinned Parzival. Both boys must make their way through life without a father to guide, support, and nurture them.

The man that life gives a boy to be his father plays a very important role in helping him develop his self-image and the sense of his own authority. When we look closely at a man's life, we can see the effects of positive, negative, or absent fathering. Over the past fifteen years I have spoken to several men who were moved by a scene in the movie *A Field of Dreams*. This movie tells the story of an Iowa farmer who hears messages from deceased baseball players and responds by building a baseball field in an Iowa cornfield for them. The scene that moved these men so deeply, and some of them to tears, is not the one where the former major-leaguers realize their dream of playing baseball again, but the scene where Ray Kinsella (played by Kevin Costner) plays catch with his father John, who died years before. In the scene Ray's father, a former minor league catcher, comes to the baseball field that Ray built. John does not recognize his son who is now a man. He asks Ray, "Is this heaven?" "No," Ray replies, "it's Iowa." They continue a short conversation, throughout which Ray calls his father "John." As the conversation ends, John turns and walks toward the cornfield where he will disappear again. However, Ray calls out to him, "Hey...Dad?" John turns. Choking up, Ray asks, "Do you wanna have a catch?" His dad replies, "I'd like that." The two men play catch, and Ray experiences what he missed as a boy—time playing with his father.

This movie scene touched something very deep in the men who talked to me about it—a hunger and longing for connection with their fathers. In my many years as a psychotherapist, I have seen in most men a deep longing to connect with their fathers. I know that longing in myself. Many of us carry a secret emptiness within us—an emptiness that we do not know how to share with other men. Too many men in this culture long to receive their father's blessing—a blessing they were meant to receive in their childhood. When a father's blessing is missing, men spend a tremendous amount of emotional energy and time, well into their adult years, trying to get what they missed.

How does a father give his blessing to his son? When a father shows his son that he sees him as he truly is and demonstrates that he is pleased with what he sees in his son, then the son receives the blessing. No one bestows this blessing in a momentary interaction, but over time in regular and consistent actions. To bless his son, a father must be present—not just physically present but emotionally present and attentive to his son and the life he is expressing. A boy will know he is blessed by his father when he feels accepted without question by his dad. When this acceptance extends beyond the times of success, especially to the times of mistakes and failures, a boy knows that the blessing is real. A sense of a father's appreciation and approval of his son can be expressed through words like, "I'm proud of you," "I really respect you for that," and "I know you can do it." However, what is more important, a boy is blessed when his father freely expresses his warmth and regard for him through affection. Our bodies receive information and meaning at a deeper level than words can communicate. When a father touches a boy with love or comforts him when he is sad or scared, the boy knows that he is safe in this chaotic world because he has his dad to lean on.

An additional way in which a father blesses his son is by setting clear, firm, and reasonable limits. A wise father knows that healthy limits help the son learn to tame his animal nature so that he can use it in a creative and healthy way. Without good limits a boy spends too much time testing his environment and is never really able to focus on developing his natural self within the environment. Lack of limits creates anxiety and worry in a boy. On the other hand, too repressive and restrictive limits crush a boy's natural spirit and later in life leaves him dependent on father figures to tell him what is acceptable. Recently one of my clients told me about his six-year-old grandson who, when his father was setting a limit, said to him, "Dad, I know you have to have your rules, but I can't let them stop my creativity." That boy had it right and he has a father who delighted in his son's openness and precociousness. This boy is receiving his father's blessing.

Was your father able to pass his blessing onto you? If you can say yes, you are one of the lucky ones. Many of us had less than desirable father experiences, not because our fathers are bad men, but because a social and religious culture that emphasizes achievement, success, and perfection wounded and limited them, instead of teaching them the value of emotional relatedness and the importance of a father's non-critical presence. My experience of working with families shows me that most fathers do the best they know how to do, but they have a difficult time giving what they themselves lacked. It takes an enormous amount of consciousness and determination to change the patterns of emotional neglect and violence that have been past down from generation to generation between fathers and sons. I am happy to report that I know many men today who are facing the pain of their own lack of healthy fathering so that they can now give to their children a healthy experience of a father's blessing.

Unfortunately some men experience not only the lack of the father's blessing, but also the father's curse. A father curses his son by words or looks that are degrading, derogatory, and disapproving. When a father tells his son that he is worthless, or stupid, or that he will never amount to anything, he is putting his curse on his son. When a father acts out his own self-loathing by emotionally or physically beating his son, he has placed his curse on him. A curse is a wicked thing for a boy to bear. With some difficult healing work and love any man can learn to free himself from a father's curse. To do so he must discover within himself the resources to bless himself and to live his own creative life. However, a father who curses his son bears the responsibility to acknowledge his failure and to do all in his power to make amends for his misdeed. It is never too late for a father to bless his son.

A father's blessing or curse is so critical because it affects the self image of his son. If a son receives his father's blessing, he will know at his core that he is loveable and competent. His life will manifest this blessing in creative and loving actions; he will live his life from an inner authority. However, if the father's blessing is missing, the boy will wonder deep inside whether he is loveable and competent—a nagging self-doubt lives in him. When a boy experiences not enough blessing, he carries a deficit throughout his life. He longs for something missing and will unconsciously seek these missing experiences through others. He may seek affection and reassurance from his partner and react angrily when she does not fill his emptiness. Some men relinquish their own journey to serve another man's vision, unconsciously seeking the approval of the missing father.

If a son receives a father's curse, he will believe that he is not loveable and not competent. His life will manifest this false belief in self-destructive and self-sabotaging behavior. A father's curse is a horrible hole out of which a boy must eventually learn to dig himself. The movie, *Walk the Line*, tells the story of the musician Johnny Cash. When Johnny was a boy, his older brother was tragically killed in a wood milling accident. Johnny loved his brother and his death devastated him. Nevertheless, his verbally abusive father acted out his pain on Johnny. One day he hatefully told Johnny that God had taken the wrong son. The father's curse was firmly placed on his son. Much of the rest of the movie documents Johnny's life of addiction, broken relationships, and self-destructive behavior. Eventually through the love of others and an enormous amount of suffering, Johnny pries himself out from under his father's curse, learns to bless himself, and lives a creative life.

Whatever our experience of our father has been, it helped to form our image of us. We create our lives out of our self image. It becomes our responsibility as men to accept our experience of our fathers as our fate and to learn to live our adult lives in a loving, empowered, and authentic way.

Our experience of our personal fathers will greatly influence how we relate to the societal father. Institutions, governments, organizations, and corporations serve as social fathers for us. They are the status quo and the authority in our lives. If a man has received his father's blessing, he will relate to these societal fathers in a way that respects and accepts their traditions and wisdom and yet he will find a way to make his own unique contribution and to create the changes that the organization needs. When a father's blessing is missing, a man lacks his own inner authority. Therefore, his relationships to the social fathers—church, government, or corporations—are dependent and powerless. While hoping to gain the ever elusive "I'm proud of you" from these surrogate fathers, he sacrifices his life and soul for the good of their cause, never risking disapproval. Many organizations and institutions thrive off the souls of such men. These organizations are the fathers who figuratively eat their own children for the sake of their cause, be it financial, civic, or religious. A man without his father's blessing is ill-equipped to see and resist this parasitic drain of his own psychic and spiritual resources.

While some men who missed the father's blessing dependently submit to these social fathers, others rebel against them. By using anger to mask their own lack of inner authority, these men fight against any authority. No one can tell them what to do. They really cannot distinguish between healthy and unhealthy authority. They must distrust and fight all authority. Despite the external appearance, these rebels are also dependent. They must be against whatever the authority wants and therefore, they are not really free to decide their own authentic response to a situation. These men are angry because they missed their father's blessing and act out their pain by attempting to sabotage the father's work wherever they can.

When a father's blessing is missing, a man struggles to find his inner authority. Whether through compliance or rebellion, he will live out this deficit in the world of the fathers.

Besides our personal fathers and our social fathers, each of us must come to understand and deal with the archetype of the father within our own psyche. Archetypes are psychic energies that are common to all people and carry a very strong emotional charge. To experience an archetype is like encountering the force of the gods within ourselves. The father archetype is the inner authority, the one who passes judgement on our life. Like all archetypes, the father archetype has its positive and negative side. The positive father archetype gives us permission to embrace life and to live it fully. When we experience the positive side, it is like receiving God's blessing on our lives; we know that we are cared for and are loveable to the core of our being. We can honestly love ourselves and we feel empowered to enter the world and fight for life.

While the positive father archetype blesses, supports, and guides us, the negative father archetype can attack, criticize, and crush us. The negative father archetype is the inner judge who renders his crippling verdict upon our life. We have all heard this name-calling voice inside us. The negative father archetype tells us that we are unworthy, inadequate, incompetent, and unlovable. It is the rule-maker within our own psyche that limits our life and creativity with its "thou shalt and thou shalt nots." We often feel condemned and powerless to combat the verdict of the negative father archetype. The experience of the negative father archetype is like receiving God's curse on our life. It is a very powerful force within our psyche that we can learn to combat. However, first we must acknowledge that this judgement is in us and it can paralyze us. When a man's personal father does not bless him, his psyche is more susceptible to being controlled by the negative father archetype and overcoming this negative force in his own psyche is more difficult.

To be conscious and free, a man must learn to hold the powerful messages from both the positive and negative father archetype until the tension between the two transforms him by bringing a new awareness of whom he is at the core of his being. To do so is to become a Parzival. Often a man will have a dream that will mark this transformation. Some men dream of the birth of a male child—a new part of himself that is awaking. I know a man who dreamed that he was in a church community where he was to cast the deciding vote for the community's leader. He voted for the woman candidate. When he did, an angry patriarch stormed in to attack him. The man faced the angry and critical father in the center of the church and did not yield to the patriarch's challenge. The dream shows that this man was coming to embrace his own authority and was placing his vote behind the feminine principle in his psyche. He was learning to stand up against the tyrannical negative father archetype within himself and to embrace a new way of relating to the world.

Coming to terms with the lives of our parents and their impact upon our lives are the first great adventures each man must face. For better or worse, how our parents lived their lives greatly influences our formation and foundation. For a man to understand himself fully and live his own authentic life, he must first come to terms with his experience of his parents. Parzival's father, Gahmuret, was killed in battle before he was born. As we will see, having an absent father will be a great challenge for Parzival to overcome. The following questions ask you to examine your relationship with your father and his impact and influence on your life.

The Questions

1. Imagine that Wolfram was writing the tale of your life and that the first chapter described your father.
    What events, character traits, successes, and failures would he include?
2. Describe how your father related or did not relate to you.
3. Describe how your father related or did not relate to your mother.
4. What did you learn from your father about aggression and assertion?
5. What did you learn from your father about sexuality?
6. Describe how you relate to authority, the laws of the land, and the status quo?
7. Describe how you relate to your culture's image of a Supreme Being.
8. How are you like your father?
9. How are you different from your father?
10. Do you remember when you surpassed your father in some area?
    What was that like for you? What was that like for him?
11. Whether he is still living or not, what do you still need to say to your father?
    Say it by writing him a letter.
12. Notice the male characters in your dreams. What are their characteristics?
    How do you interact with them in your dream? How do they interact with you?

Chapter Two

The Mother
Inner Life

Why is it important to have an inner life and why is it important to pay attention to our dreams? A rich, valuable, and a much-neglected world exists within each of us. Within this world we have resources that can renew and sustain us when our lives become overwhelmed with activity or stress, that is, when we find ourselves living in the Waste Land. The key to these resources is within us. Discovering this hidden treasure is the search we are undertaking in this book. It is our search for the Grail.

The discussion of the inner life that will be presented in this book is based on the psychology of C.G. Jung. Dr. Jung taught that to understand a human personality one had to see the spiritual nature of the individual. As he studied his own dreams and his patients' dreams, Jung saw a pattern. He discovered that within the psyche a force challenges and pushes the individual toward wholeness. Individuation is the name Jung gave to the life long process of the unfolding of our authentic personality—the person we were born to become. Because of this discovery, Jung taught that the unconscious consists not only of repressed material, but that in the unconscious there also lives an Other. This Other is an organizing center, different from one's conscious identity. Jung called this Other reality, the Self. The Self is not a thing inside us, but the Self is a metaphor for a process: the constant extension and the constant maturing of the personality. Jung used the idea of the acorn and the oak tree to explain this idea. He taught that the oak tree is an individuated acorn. Within the acorn the potential oak tree lives. With the right conditions, that is, in the ground, with the proper sunlight and rain, and if it can avoid the bulldozers of progress, the oak tree will emerge from the acorn. This process happens naturally and automatically.

As human beings both our awareness of our true nature and our choices are essential for the individuation process. We are like the acorn when we are born. Within us is a seed—the germ of whom we really are as a unique human being. Not every one of us will necessarily develop into our authentic self—our true nature. This is true, partially because of our personal history, but more importantly because of what we do with our history and the choices we make. Every choice matters in this process: the littlest ones and the biggest ones. The right relationship between my conscious self and this bigger Self is essential. The story of Parzival addresses the tasks of learning how to relate to the Self and by that become one's truest self. In this story, we are watching the personality of the hero grow and evolve. We will see the twists and the turns, the wrong roads taken, the help given, the heartaches, and the courageous choices that are necessary for the unfolding of an authentic self. Parzival is a boy who does not know his father. His responses to this fact of his history and the choices he makes determine whether he can reach the Grail. The evolution of his personality in this story develops in three steps: from Innocence, through Doubt, to Soulfulness.[1] Soulfulness is Parzival's coming to the awareness of whom he truly is and living from that reality. By following Parzival's life, we will see how he experiences his own process of individuation.

Our awareness of the reality of the Self is essential. For instance, we may be naturally gifted in science, music, human relations, or mechanics. When someone in our lives recognizes our gift, it naturally begins to unfold. Usually our parents are the first to see or ignore our gifts. We need someone to see us and we need to experience ourselves being seen by another. The experience of being seen gives energy to our natural self. When no one sees our natural self or when someone criticizes it, our life force diminishes. Our natural self begins to shrivel and disappear. We then develop a false self or a provisional self and we will consequently live in a way that is adaptive to our environment. For example, we may become a pleaser, a doer, a performer, an over-giver, or a rebel to have worth or value in our environment. When we live from a provisional self, much of our true and natural self remains buried and we do not even know it. Thus we live a life that is out of accord with our truest nature—and in doing so we create our personal Waste Land.

The best parenting sees and mirrors a child's natural self and then nourishes that soul as it naturally evolves. As we mature, our task is to see our own soul and to help it evolve. Inner work and dream work are ways of discovering a deeper and clearer picture of our own nature. If we learn to develop a relationship with our inner world, we begin to realize that we have a soul that wants to be expressed. Like Sigune in the Parzival story, we have an inner reality that gives direction, tells us its opinion, and gives correction to us by means of dreams. The task of consciousness is to realize that an inner soul-reality exists, to listen to its messages, and then to apply its wisdom to our current conscious life. To do inner work is not merely engaging in introspection for its own sake—it is not egotism. Inner work enables us to discover our authentic self and to become a vessel through which that authentic self is expressed in the world. As we accomplish this task, we are experiencing individuation.

Through the individuation process, the personality becomes healthy and vital and open to creative energy. When we thwart or deny our individuation, life becomes meaningless and we experience worries, addictions, depression, and broken relations. In other words, we are in the Waste Land, and our inner Grail King is wounded and in need of healing. The wounded King means that the connection between our conscious self and the Self is broken. When this connection is broken, we create our life out of this disconnected reality and our personal Waste Land is a testimony to this disconnection. The Gnostic Gospel of Thomas expresses this truth when it quotes Jesus as saying:

When you know your Selves
then you will be known,
and you will be aware that you are
the sons (and daughters) of the Living Father.
But if you do not know yourselves
then you live in poverty
and you are the poverty. (logion 3)

Psychologically speaking, to be aware that we are a son or a daughter of the Living Father means that we are aware that the Self is operating within and through us. The proper response to this reality is to ask what the Self is engineering in our lives, to yield to it, and then to serve its truth. However, when we are unaware of the Self operating in our lives, we live in poverty—our lives are without soul and we are the poverty.

We will see the process of individuation unfold in the story of Parzival. Individuation is our goal and inner work is an important tool for the evolution of our souls. Now let us return to Parzival's life. We will see how his mother raised him without her husband and how that influenced the development of his personality. Despite his mother's well-intentioned efforts to protect him, Parzival had a unique personality and life force that he could not deny. His inner Self will challenge him to go beyond the world in which he was raised and into the world of his true destiny.

The Story and Commentary

Herzeloyde is two weeks from giving birth to Parzival when she hears the news of her husband's death. She has already lost one husband to knightly combat and now a second. She can hardly bear this pain and she contemplates suicide. However, the child in her womb, Gahmuret's child, becomes her reason for living. In the midst of his mother's grief, Parzival is born. When Herzeloyde sees her newborn son, her maternal instinct transforms her sorrow. She becomes determined to protect Parzival from the horrors of combat, because her heart cannot bear another loss. Then, she leaves her village with her servants and travels to a primitive country forest. There she raises her precious Parzival in peace. Herzeloyde forbids her servants ever to speak to her boy of knighthood and warfare. By doing so she attempts to guarantee Parzival's safety.

The forest village is an idyllic place for Parzival to spend his formative years. Over time Herzeloyde's grief fades. Raising her son in peace and beauty gives meaning to her life. She calls Parzival by his pet name, "bon fils, cher fils, beau fils," that is, "good son, dear son, beautiful son." All is lovely and tranquil for Herzeloyde and Parzival.

However, Parzival has his father's blood in him. As a young child, he made little bows, arrows, and javelins for play. He is also a child of nature and spends hours entranced by the singing of birds. One day he shoots an arrow at a singing bird and not knowing the effects of such an action kills the bird. Because Parzival is a sensitive boy, he immediately begins to weep at the loss of the beautiful song of the bird. For the next several days, whenever he would hear the singing of a bird, Parzival would burst into tears. Herzeloyde cannot stand to see her son in pain and she orders her servants to trap every bird they can find and wring their necks. Parzival asks her why she would stop the birds from singing their beautiful songs. Herzeloyde, suddenly realizing what she has done, says, "Why should I alter His commandment Who is, after All, Supreme God? Should birds lose their delight because of me?"[2] Parzival then asks, "What is God?"—a critical question for any child to ask. Herzeloyde begins to tell him her spiritual beliefs. God, she says, is the brightest of all light and one must pray to God and not kneel before anyone, except God. She warns Parzival that a master of darkness also exists and one must fight against darkness. This conversation is Parzival's earliest spiritual teaching. We are already seeing the enormous influence Parzival's mother has on his early life, but we are also noticing that Parzival has other forces in his life that Herzeloyde cannot control.

In his protective environment, Parzival grows into a splendid adolescent. He is strong and very handsome. He becomes an excellent hunter. Parzival brings down many deer with his javelin and with his strength he carries them home on his back. However, life will not allow Parzival to remain in this state of innocence. His destiny is about to pay him a call.

One day while he is in the forest hunting, Parzival hears a noise. He thinks to himself that maybe he will run into the devil so that he can fight him and by that please his mother. Parzival is truly a good boy. Of course, it is not the devil, but three knights who have entered the forest. They are chasing another knight who has kidnaped a damsel. This sight spellbinds Parzival, as he has never seen a knight before. He sees the knights' armor glistening in the sunlight, and thinks that he must be seeing the god of whom his mother spoke. Immediately Parzival kneels before them—right in the middle of the road. Just then a fourth knight, a partner of the other three, rides upon the scene of this youth kneeling in the road. He stops and Parzival begins to pray to him. The knight tells him that he is not a god and orders Parzival to get up. Since he is not a god, Parzival asks him what he is. The man tells him that he is a knight. The moment most feared by Herzeloyde has arrived. Parzival asks what a knight is and how one becomes a knight. They tell him that Arthur makes knights and that he must go to Arthur's court and, if found worthy, Arthur will make him a knight. Parzival is spellbound and the idea of knighthood becomes the driving force of his life for many years to come. The knights' armor greatly fascinates Parzival. He thinks to himself that, if the deer wore this armor, his javelins would never have killed them. Because of meeting the knights, Parzival forever loses interest in hunting deer. Becoming a knight is all about which he cares.

Parzival runs back to Herzeloyde and tells her the whole story of meeting the knights, and most importantly that he wants to become a knight. Herzeloyde, realizing the full impact of the moment, is so overwhelmed that she faints. When she recovers, she hears Parzival begging her for a horse. She knows that she can neither refuse him nor talk him out of this idea. Therefore, she develops a plan to foil her son's notion of becoming a knight. She fashions a garment out of sackcloth and leather footwear for him. This outfit was the clothing worn by the fools of the time. She tells Parzival that she has made special clothes for him to wear on his journey to Arthur's court. Then for his horse she gets the oldest, most run-down nag she can find. Secretly, she hopes that people will laugh and discourage Parzival from becoming a knight. However, Parzival is thrilled to be outfitted, as he sees it, in such a splendid manner.

The next morning Parzival gets dressed in the homespun garment from his mother and mounts the nag. Before he leaves, Herzeloyde gives him some parting advice: do not ride through deep water, be polite and greet all people in the name of God, and if a wise, grey-haired man offers to teach him manners, he ought to do as he says. Finally about women she says, "Whenever you can win a good woman's ring and greeting, take them; it will set you free of cares. You must make haste to kiss her and clasp her tight in your embrace. This brings happiness and a stout spirit, if she is chaste and good."[3] Then she tells him the truth about his origins: his father was Gahmuret whose kingdoms are now under siege by a Duke named **Orilus**. Parzival listens closely to his mothers parting words and holds them close to his heart.

Parzival begins a journey that will eventually lead him to the Grail Castle in a most inauspicious manner. He rides on the old nag and he wears the clothes of a fool. However in his mind he is ready to avenge the loss of his father's land and to find Arthur's court. Parzival begins his journey as an innocent, naive, young man with grand plans. Most men, if they are honest with themselves, will admit that they began their life away from home as innocent, naive, and well-meaning young men, but without a real sense of what life held in store for them.

Herzeloyde watches Parzival's image fade away and, with a heart already too full of sorrow, collapses and dies. What a start to a boy's journey! Parzival's choice to leave home, as necessary as it is, kills his mother. He is totally unaware of this fact. However, as we can see, intense forces are converging as the young Parzival starts this phase of his life's journey.

After leaving his mother, Parzival rides the run-down nag until he comes to a river. Vegetation that makes it impossible for Parzival to see the depth of the water surrounds the river. Remembering his mother's advice to avoid deep water, Parzival follows it for a whole day, not daring to cross. When he finally gets to a spot without vegetation, he sees how shallow it is and he crosses. Wolfram tells us that a chicken could have easily crossed it at any point. In this scene we see the effects of the lack of fathering on Parzival—his inability confidently to negotiate his path away from home. A father who is present teaches his son the necessary skills to face the challenges of the world. Parzival lacks these skills for now. However, his determination to become a knight is strong enough to push him forward.

After crossing the river Parzival discovers a tent. A young woman named **Jeshute** is in the tent. She is the wife of Orilus, the man who has taken his father's land. However, Parzival knows nothing of this. He goes into the tent and sees that she is sleeping. Then, remembering his mother's advice about women and taking it literally, he leaps upon her bed, embraces her, and kisses her. This action startles Jeshute; she is surprised to awaken to this fool accosting her. She pushes him away. Parzival takes her ring and a brooch—just like his mother told him to do, or so he thought. Since Parzival is hungry, he devours her bread and drinks her wine. Then he hastily leaves her with the greeting, "God shield you as my mother told me to say." He has not had any experience with a woman, besides his mother. Parzival's first experience with a woman is probably not unlike most men's first encounter with a woman—very clumsy.

Soon after Parzival's departure from Jeshute's tent, Orilus returns to his wife. He sees the horse tracks and a man's footprints into the tent. Orilus is convinced that Jeshute has been unfaithful to him. Although she tells him the story of this simpleton coming to her tent and accosting her, she cannot convince Orilus otherwise. Therefore, he forces Jeshute to ride behind him on an old nag and to wear the clothes of a penitent as her punishment for her perceived unfaithfulness. Of course, Parzival again knows nothing of the consequences of his actions. Nevertheless, as the story unfolds, he must make this situation right and become responsible for the effects of his actions on Jeshute.

Parzival rides on, and still dressed like a fool, comes upon a terrible scene. From behind a bush he hears the wailing of a woman. He rides over to investigate. He finds a woman who is holding on her lap the corpse of her recently-murdered, beloved knight. The woman is Sigune, whom we discussed in the introduction as the grieving, human soul. The dead man on her lap is a knight who rode with Parzival's father and became his right-hand man. Again, Parzival is oblivious to this. He greets her and asks about her situation. She tells him that the dead knight is her beloved who was killed in a jousting match. She then focuses on Parzival and asks him his name. Parzival responds, "They call me bon fils, cher fils, beau fils." Sigune immediately recognizes his mother in his voice. Sigune is Herzeloyde's niece. Herzeloyde raised her for a time, because Sigune's mother died in childbirth. Sigune tells Parzival that his real name is Parzival and that it means "right through the middle."

As stated earlier, besides being an actual character that is weeping because of the death of her beloved, inwardly Sigune also represents Parzival's soul grieving because of his disconnection from her. Every man who is the seeker of his authentic self must some day meet his Sigune—his grieving soul, for she is the one within him who knows his identity. She grieves for him until the day he embraces his true self and begins to live his own authentic life. As we will see, Sigune will reappear three more times in our tale. Each time by her demeanor she will show Parzival's relationship to his true nature and path. In this first meeting we see symbolically that Parzival is disconnected from his soul—he is dead to her. One cannot imagine this scene without also thinking of the Pietá, the sculpture by Michelangelo in which his mother is holding Jesus after his death.

Sigune also tells Parzival that her beloved was killed by Orilus—the same man who, unbeknownst to Parzival, is angrily pursuing him for dishonoring Jeshute. In fact, we find out that Sigune's beloved was killed while defending Parzival's land and that Orilus believed that he was jousting with Gahmuret's son. Therefore, in a very real way this knight, whom Sigune is holding in her lap, died for Parzival.

Upon hearing Sigune's story of the death of her beloved, Parzival wants to avenge the wrong done to her by finding Orilus and doing battle with him. But Sigune, knowing that Parzival is too untrained to stand a chance against Orilus, sends him in the opposite direction. I once heard Robert Johnson say that life, instead of being two steps forward and one back, is really one step forward and two back. "But that is good," he said, "because we are usually going the wrong way anyway." The ego-self wants to go one way and the Self has a different direction in which to send us. The Self's way is the correct way for the development of our soul. Fortunately for Parzival he listens to Sigune and heads in the wrong direction, which turns out to be the right direction for him.

In this segment of the story we see Parzival's first experience with women, especially how his mother influenced and formed him. The mother plays a very important role in the psyche of every man, more than most of us would care to admit. When we are children, we experience our mother as an awesome, life-giving or life-threatening power. Her behavior, her emotions, and her demeanor set our expectations about life. If she is safe and nurturing, we will approach life with openness and trust. If she is emotionally absent, critical, or invasive, we will approach life with hesitation, self-doubt, and fearfulness. The woman that life gives us as our mother helps form our expectations of women and of all things feminine.

For any man who wishes to take his life seriously it is critical to know and accept how his mother influenced and formed him. It is essential that he knows and is thankful for the positive influences that he received from his mother. Likewise, knowing the weaknesses and vulnerabilities that he has inherited because of her shortcomings or failures is important for him. By that, he can work with his own vulnerabilities and honestly face the challenges of his life, especially as they appear in his relationships with women. I know a man whose mother was so determined to raise him to be appropriate and to make her look good that he felt completely unseen by her and was suspicious that every interaction contained her agenda for him. Now as an adult not only does he hold his mother at arms length, but he has a very difficult time maintaining a close and trusting relationship with a woman. When a woman expresses her desires or interests, he is quick to interpret them as her desire to control and possess him. This man has several options. He can accept that he has an understandable fear of being controlled by a woman and work on developing his own internal self-acceptance and strength so that he is able confidently to relate to a woman as an equal where both his and her wishes matter. Or he can refuse to face the influence of his mother and continue to act out his hurt, suspicion, and anger of his childhood with the women in his adult life. In this way his experience of his mother is unconsciously still controlling him and he has not grown up.

I know another man whose mother was a kind woman who did all the necessary functions of a mother. She washed his clothes, fed him well, anticipated his needs, prepared him for school, and drove him to his sporting events. He had a good mother. Despite her unselfish giving to her son and to his siblings, this mother was emotionally shut down and uncomfortable with her emotional self. Therefore, her son could not experience an emotional connection with her in his body. It is not that she did not love him, it was that her heart was shut down and her son could not bond with her there. As her son became an adult, he found himself emotionally dependent in relationships with women. He feared that they would leave him or that no matter how much they shared themselves with him, he still felt something was lacking. After a series of broken relationships in which he became controlling and demanding, this man began to see the problem within himself instead of in the women in his life. He began to honestly look at his experience as a boy, recognize and accept that he had an emotional emptiness inside himself that he needed to grieve. Eventually, he was able to find ways of healing this pain by finding inner resources that could fill his loneliness and his lack of belief in his own worthiness to be loved. This change has allowed him to live in harmony and love with his wife.

Just as we saw in the previous chapter, the experience of the father takes place for us not only on the personal level but also on the social level, so too with our experience of the mother. Institutions, organizations, and corporations serve as mothers for us in as much as they are containers that hold us and help give us a sense of identity and belonging. If a man has not come to terms with his own need for positive and healthy mothering inside himself, he will find himself unconsciously attempting to resolve this problem by either allowing himself to be possessed by these organizations or endlessly fighting against them.

Finally, the deepest level of the mother experience is the archetype of mother. The mother archetype is a strong force in a man's psyche. On the positive side the mother archetype gives us a deep sense of love, acceptance, and understanding. The positive mother archetype, sometimes called the Great Mother, is the experience of the universal sense of being surrounded and supported by the nurturing force of life. Special moments in life give us a glimpse of this reality that is always available for us. The experience of the Great Mother can come in experiences of nature—a sunset or a walk in the woods. We experience this archetype in times of creativity, whether we are a writer, an artist, a machinist, or a carpenter. Special life moments, such as the birth of a child, a moment of prayer, or making love to our partner, can give us a connection to a deep truth about life. The experience of the Great Mother is the experience of heaven on earth. One of the most helpful descriptions of this experience is found in *The Ravaged Bridegroom* by Marion Woodman in which she describes the experience of the Great Mother as:

>...the primal wisdom that assures us that we are loved,that life is our birthright, that we need not prove ourselves nor justify our existence. Knowing in our bones that life is the supreme gift, we can accept paradox. Life is no longer broken into right and wrong, light and dark, birth or death. Everything is part of the awesome mystery. [4]

To experience the Great Mother is to experience the Grail. Parzival, like many of us, is searching for an experience of the Great Mother without knowing it. Deep down we all want to experience that a power greater than ourselves unconditionally loves us. As we get to know ourselves and our inner world, we can discover that the Great Mother is alive within us.

All archetypes have two sides. The other side of the Great Mother is the negative mother archetype. As wonderful and life-giving as the Great Mother is, so the negative mother archetype is equally destructive and harmful to a man's desire for a meaningful and creative life. We are all too familiar with this experience. The negative mother is the inner experience of criticism. She is the feeling we have within us that we are not good enough or that something is inherently wrong with us. Often this belief in our unworthiness is unconscious and it sabotages our efforts to live a creative, healthy life. I know a man who was divorced for ten years and had resigned himself to a single life. One day he met a woman with whom he fell in love. After an initial time of closeness and bliss, he suddenly and unexplainably became suspicious of his new girlfriend. He began to fear that she was attracted to other men and was intending to cheat on him. He became very critical and controlling. Naturally this reaction caused some major arguments between himself and his girlfriend. She had no designs to find other men and was baffled and hurt by his attacks. It was this man's internal negative mother archetype that was telling him that no one could really love him, that other men would be much better for his girlfriend, that she could not be trusted, and many other self-sabotaging ideas. He was experiencing a great inner torture and he was acting it out with the woman he loved. The negative mother archetype was destroying his love—desiring to keep him alone and isolated. Unfortunately, this man could not find the courage nor the will to face his internal torment. Eventually, his attacks drove away the woman he loved.

As we get to know ourselves, we see that the negative mother archetype really does live in us. We all have to wrestle with the reality of self-criticism and self-devaluation and learn to come to dis-identify from it. Working with our dreams can show us when the force of the negative mother is unconsciously operating in our lives. We will explore this idea in the following chapters.

As Wolfram says, we are all like the magpie. Within us we all have the white feathers of the Great Mother and the black feathers of the negative mother. We are encouraged to be the Parzival—the one who comes to know both sides of his nature without denying either, and the one who can freely choose to live a meaningful, productive, and loving life.

Another aspect of the mother archetype is portrayed beautifully in the Parzival story. When he begins his journey to become a knight,

Parzival wears the garment that his mother fashioned for him. He wears the clothing worn by the fools of his day. Parzival's Fool's Clothing is symbolic of his mother complex.[5] The mother complex is the regressive tendency in every person and it is one of the most difficult attitudes for a man to face on his journey toward a healthy and authentic life. In fact, the mother complex is one of the biggest impediments to full maturity and manhood. When a man is caught in his mother complex, he is symbolically wearing the Fool's Clothing. For some men the mother complex can be seen when he is avoiding the necessary confrontation of a problem or situation in life—it is his inactivity and passivity. The mother complex is a man's desire to be taken care of by someone else. For many men we see this in their marriages where they expect their partner to be mother to them, that is, to anticipate their every need, to always be present and available, and especially to fulfill all their sexual desires. We know we are wearing the Fool's Clothing in our marriages when we react with anger, control, withdrawal, and silent punishment when our partner fails to live up to this prescribed role.

The mother complex can also be seen in the man who evades responsibility and refuses to acknowledge his own role in a problem by blaming someone else for his behaviors and failings. That man is wearing the Fool's Clothing. When a man gives into the mother complex, he is losing the battle of life. By that he becomes defeated and impotent.

Finally, the mother complex can be masked in a man who over identifies with responsibility. Since he wishes to look good in other people's eyes, this type of man becomes too responsible by assuming obligation for everything. If someone in his life is distressed, he feels obliged to fix it. He will take over projects and not allow others to complete them in their own way. Others will eventually experience this seeming generous man as controlling and manipulating. The man himself will often harbor a growing resentment toward those he feels obliged to act as caretaker. This man's task is not to learn to be responsible, but to learn which responsibilities are his to take up and which ones are his to relinquish.

All men must struggle with the Fool's Clothing and the attitude that it represents. The first step toward freedom is to acknowledge that the problem is an attitude within me. If I can accept the mother complex as an internal matter, then I can begin to honestly ask myself several pointed questions. Where am I expecting someone else to take care of me? Where am I expecting someone else to be responsible for something that is really mine to deal with? Where do I blame others for my problems? Where am I shirking my responsibilities? Where am

I taking up someone else's responsibilities? Where am I afraid to live who I know I really am? If one can honestly answer these questions and then choose to take up his own life and responsibilities, he will come a long way in overcoming the force of the mother complex. He will be removing his Fool's Clothing.

Throughout this story we will watch Parzival wrestle with his Fool's Clothing and attempt to remove them. It is important for Parzival not only literally to take off the Fool's Clothing, but also to take off the attitude they represent. When we return to Parzival and we will see how the Fool's Clothing affects his journey.

Before following Parzival on the next steps of his journey, we pause to reflect upon our relationship to our mother. In the questions we will be examining not only our relationship with our personal mother, but also our relationship with our societal mother and the archetypal mother in its various forms.

The Questions

1. Describe your mother. What events formed her personality? What were her strengths and weaknesses as a mother?

2. Describe how your mother related to you.

3. Describe how your mother related to your father and to other men.

4. What did your mother teach you about women—either verbally or by her actions?

5. Where was your mother on the spectrum between overprotective and emotionally absent?
   How was that for you?

6. Did your mother shame you? If so, how did you respond?

7. Did your mother teach you any spiritual truths? What are they? How did this affect you?

8. When do you get taken over by your mother complex? How are you doing at taking off the Fool's Clothing?

9. How do you relate to "mother church," "mother university," and "mother corporation"?

10. Have you had the experience of being deeply accepted (the Great Mother)?
    What helps you to nurture or develop this?

11. Are you aware of your own self-criticism? How do you deal with that negative mother archetype?

12. What experiences or people have helped you discover your true nature? How has this affected you?

13. Notice the female characters in your dreams. How do you relate to them? How do they relate to you?

Chapter Three

The Red Knight
Inner Life

An excellent way to begin focusing on the inner world is to record your dreams. Many men tell me that they do not dream or that they rarely remember their dreams. Remembering dreams is difficult because so much of our training in the Western culture focuses on the real world, that is, the outer life. Consequently and unfortunately, we see our inner world of imagination, emotions, and dreams as secondary or unimportant. We do not naturally see the value of the inner world. Therefore, we need some time and experiences to learn its value and to be able to recall our dreams consistently. Most people find it helpful to place a pen and notebook by their bed before going to sleep. By doing so, they set their intention to record any dream they remember. Upon waking they ask themselves, "Did I have a dream?" and, if so, they write down whatever they remember without editing or interpreting. One man told me that when he asked himself if he could remember a dream, he would always get nothing. However, if he spent several more moments quietly in bed before rushing into his day and then he asked the question again, he began to recall the dream. Each person should experiment and find the method that works for him or her. My experience is that when a person sincerely seeks to know himself through the dream world, the unconscious will respond with its voice, the dreams.

The primary purpose of recalling and then working with my dreams is to get to know myself better. The more that I know myself, the more choices and options I have in my life. I will experience more freedom and will discover ways of living that are expressions of my natural self—instead of living in the "poverty" of unconsciousness. C. G. Jung states that what we do not deal with consciously comes to us as fate. This is a startling idea. What he means is that what we do not know about ourselves controls us. For instance, if a man did not have his emotional needs adequately responded to as a boy, he will likely come to the conclusion that he is not really loveable—although this conclusion may remain unconscious. When this boy grows up, he takes a job and begins a family. Consciously he thinks to himself that he is an average guy. However, if unconsciously he believes that he is unlovable, this belief will begin to manifest in his life especially in his relationships. He will unconsciously draw into his life people and events that will give him the experience of rejection—not because he is unlovable, but because he believes unconsciously that he is. What he does not deal with consciously now comes to him as fate, that is, it comes to him in outer life experiences. If someone had taught him how to listen to his dreams, he may have confronted this false belief about himself and he may have addressed this problem consciously before it manifested so drastically in his relationships. Developing a relationship with my inner life helps me to know the parts of myself that have been controlling me without my knowledge. The insight that I gain will enable me to make healthier and more creative choices for my life.

Most dreams are mirrors that help us see ourselves more clearly. But some dreams are windows that help us see an outer life situation more clearly. For instance, if a man dreams that the left rear tire on his automobile is flat, it would be a good idea to check that tire in the morning. If it is low on air, then his unconscious mind noticed the tire the day before and attempted to let him know this fact before he got onto the freeway. However, if the tire were fine, then the dream image would be trying to tell him something about himself. Maybe he is more fatigued than he realizes. The dream could be warning him that he has been driving himself too hard and that he cannot continue to go at his present pace. If he understands the message of the dream, he could then make other choices to slow the pace of his life so that he does not make himself sick.

At first, learning to understand the meaning of dreams seems very difficult. Dreams seem so mysterious because they rarely speak English. They speak their own language, the language of symbols. To learn about dreams requires that we undertake the task of learning symbolic language—the language of image, symbol, and metaphor. I have experienced that most men can learn the language of dreams with a little effort and direction. In my men's groups, I ask each member to bring a symbol that represents something of his life that week. I have been impressed with how powerful this process is for men. When a man brings a rock, or a picture of himself as a boy, or a dollar bill and then tells the story that the symbol represents for him, an instantaneous and deep sharing occurs. The other men begin to know him at a deeper level and are given permission and invitation to share themselves too. After several weeks of speaking to each other through symbols, some men are surprised that they know each at a deep soul level and have not gotten around to find out if the other men are lawyers, teachers, truck drivers, or carpenters. They discover that a man is much more than what he does for a living—he is a soul. Symbols are powerful conveyers of meaning and affect; they are the language of dreams.

Dreams are a pictorial representation of what is happening in my psyche. It is as if the unconscious is saying, "Let me tell you what your life is like today...It is like..." and then it tells a story about me to get its message across. Implied in the dream is the idea that, if I were aware of the dream's message, my life would improve. The dream is always trying to tell me something I do not know about myself. It may be showing me where I might be off track or what I need to face to function in a healthier way. Most dreams contain two distinct points of view. The first point of view is that of me, the dreamer—my conscious attitude or perspective. The second point of view is that of the Self. Usually the Self's perspective is different from that of my ego and is trying to get me to expand my awareness. For example, I dream that I am walking in the jungle and a lion begins to chase me. I turn and run as fast as I can, but the lion keeps gaining on me. I wake at this point in a cold sweat and record this scene as it happened without interpretation or editing. In the morning I would ask myself what I associate with a lion. If I think a lion represents strength, power, and confidence, then the dream might be telling me that I have within myself more strength, power, and confidence than I am aware of, but that I am afraid of it and am running from it. I then look at my life and ask where I need strength and confidence but am afraid to exercise it. I might see that I have some things to discuss with my boss or my wife, but I am afraid of the consequences. Therefore, if I were to muster up my lion strength and deal with the situation directly, my life would be healthier and freer. I would not feel so ineffective and powerless in those situations. In this example the dream came to help me with my fear of asserting myself and suggested a remedy for it. This dream shows the two different points of view. The dreamer who is running from the lion has the attitude that the lion energy is dangerous and must be avoided. On the other hand, the Self wants the dreamer to see and accept his lion-self so that he can use his courageous nature to face the conflicts in his life.

The Self's perspective is always seeking to expand the dreamer's narrow perspective.

The idea that there is another point of view within us will serve as the foundation for understanding our dreams. If you recall a recent dream ask yourself what your bigger Self is trying to help you see. By doing this you may receive a new insight into yourself and you might not have to receive the message in a harsher form in your waking life. As Dr. Jung taught, what we do not deal with consciously comes to us as experiences in the outer life. What we do not deal with deals with us.

If you do not already work with your dreams, put a notebook and pen by your bed tonight and begin to act as if within you there is another reality that you do not know—a reality that is trying to help you live your life more fully.

As we return to Parzival's story, we will see that there is a reality bigger than his own ego-awareness that is guiding him on his life's journey.

The Story and Commentary

Parzival travels in the direction that Sigune suggests. He proudly rides the old nag and wears the foolish outfit that he received from his mother. His first night away from home he meets a fisherman and for a night's lodging, he trades the brooch that he stole from Jeshute. The next morning the fisherman gives him directions to Arthur's court. Parzival leaves with an intense desire burning in his chest—the desire to become a knight. He comes to a field just outside Arthur's court and discovers a most amazing sight. Standing in the field is a stunning and powerful knight. The knight's armor is red as are his shield and spear. Even his horse is adorned in red. He is the **Red Knight.** Parzival is captivated by this knight and now wants to have armor exactly like his, just as a young man wants to have a hot sports car today.

The Red Knight had just ridden into Arthur's court. He was angry with Arthur about a land dispute. To make his point, he took a goblet of wine from Arthur's table and challenged any knight to come out to the field and take the goblet from him. In his haste to steal the cup, he accidentally spilled some wine on the Queen, **Ginover.** Back in Arthur's court, the knights are confused about how to respond to this provocation. The Red Knight is a fierce warrior and no one is very interested in taking up the challenge.

Parzival greets the Red Knight, "God be with you as my mother taught me to say." The Red Knight is amused to hear such a greeting from a boy dressed like a fool and riding such a useless horse. He is even more amused to hear that Parzival is looking for Arthur because he wants to become a knight. The Red Knight points Parzival toward Arthur's court and tells him to deliver the message that he is waiting for any one of Arthur's knights to take up the challenge of a joust, and that he apologizes to the Queen for accidentally spilling the wine.

Dressed like a simpleton, Parzival rides into Arthur's court with the Red Knight's message. He first meets a page and greets him politely as his mother taught him. As Parzival surveys the court he thinks that all the knights he sees are Arthur and he wonders which one of the Arthurs will make him a knight. His naivete humors the page who takes him to the King. Parzival greets **Arthur** in the manner that his mother taught him. He delivers the message from the Red Knight and tells Arthur that not only does he want to be made a knight but that he also wants the armor that the Red Knight is wearing. The other knights have a good laugh over this request and some of them mockingly suggest that Arthur send Parzival to fight the Red Knight. Arthur fears that the Red Knight will hurt the lad but he knows someone must answer the challenge and all his knights are reluctant to face the Red Knight. So Arthur tells Parzival that, if he can defeat the Red Knight, he can have his armor. Parzival is elated and returns to the field to challenge the Red Knight.

As he is leaving Arthur's court, Parzival passes an area where many women and some men are watching him with astonishment. One of the women is **Cunneware**. Years before, she had taken an oath not to laugh again until the best and most worthy knight would arrive in the court. When she sees Parzival dressed in the Fool's Clothes and riding the old nag, she lets out a great laugh. Standing right behind her is the ill-tempered knight **Keie**. He knows the oath Cunneware has taken and he knows many great knights have come to Arthur's court. He sees Cunneware's laughter as an insult to Arthur and to his many great knights. Keie grabs Cunneware by the hair and strikes her with his staff so hard that it rips through her dress and breaks the skin on her back. Standing next to them is a dwarf whom they thought to be mute. He had vowed not to speak until Lady Cunneware laughed. Upon hearing her hearty laughter, the dwarf began to prophesy that, because of his striking Cunneware, deep sorrow would come to Keie one day. When Keie hears the dwarf's prophecy, he takes his staff and unmercifully strikes the dwarf.

We see in Keie a common but unattractive male quality. An honest man recognizes that he has a side of himself that is very ill-humored and cruel toward his inner feminine and toward the women in his life. We see this Keie-like attitude in the man who is friendly and outgoing in the workplace or social life, but who has a harsh, snappy tone toward his wife or his children. This behavior reveals a man's poor relationship with his own feminine nature. We will see how to correct this problem when we discuss the male mood in the next chapter.

When Parzival sees Keie striking Cunneware, he is very upset. He has never seen a woman treated so badly. He instinctively grabs one of his javelins with the hope of hitting Keie, just as he had hit so many a deer in his mother's forest. However, he is afraid that he might hit one of the women, so he resists his impulse. Witnessing Cunneware's mistreatment deeply troubles Parzival. Throughout the story Parzival attempts to correct the wrong done to her.

Parzival then rides out to the Red Knight and tells him that he has come to fight him for Arthur's goblet. The Red Knight has never seen such a sight and is angry that no worthy opponent has come from the court to take up his challenge. He knows he could take his spear and run Parzival right through, but instead he turns his spear around and strikes Parzival so hard with the blunt end that both Parzival and the old nag topple to the ground. Parzival is furious and quickly grabs one of his homemade javelins and hurls it at the Red Knight. The javelin travels right through the visor of the Red Knight, straight into his eye, and kills him. The Red Knight's death causes a great deal of sorrow in Arthur's court. Despite the land dispute, the Red Knight was deeply honored and respected by the court. The Red Knight is the only person whom Parzival kills in this tale, but this deed reverberates throughout the story.

This killing does not trouble Parzival; he is happy to claim the Red Knight's armor for himself. The problem is that he also knows nothing about armor and he cannot figure out how to get it off the Red Knight. The page who first met Parzival sees this disturbance in the field and comes out to investigate. He arrives at the field and finds Parzival dragging the body of the Red Knight around the field trying to get the armor off. The page helps Parzival remove the armor from the Red Knight and then helps him to put it on. Parzival wants to put the armor on over his Fool's Clothing. The page tells him to remove his ridiculous outfit. Since Parzival received these clothes from his mother, he cannot let them go. Although the page sees this as foolish, he nonetheless helps Parzival put the Red Knight's armor on over his Fool's Clothing.

Before mounting the horse Parzival asks the page to return the goblet to Arthur and to tell him that his heart is in pain for the maiden whom Keie so mistreated. The page helps Parzival to mount the Red Knight's horse. He is not used to a powerful, spirited horse. Parzival knows how to get the horse started. However, he has no idea how to stop it. So off our hero goes, hanging onto the horse for dear life. Parzival's experience with the Red Knight's horse is a metaphor of a man's experience of his instincts. When a man experiences a tremendous power for the first time, his instincts can carry him away. Substances like sex, drugs, power, and love can activate his instincts and serve as an unwieldy horse for him.

Before continuing with our story, let us examine the image of the Red Knight. The Red Knight is an instinctive energy in every man. It is his aggressiveness.[1] The Red Knight is the side of a man that takes what he wants when he wants. It is the energy that does whatever he wants, just because he wants. Learning how to relate to the tremendous force of aggression is a significant struggle for most men. The dilemma is this: if a man identifies with this force, he becomes a brute and brings much destruction to his life and to others, but if he represses it, he becomes an ineffectual wimp. Every man must face his Red Knight and learn to deal with his aggressive energy. This is a major task of adolescence. We see teenagers involved in all sorts of activities in which they experience the Red Knight. Activities such as making the team, winning the big game, climbing the mountain, or hitchhiking across the country can be experiences that help boys learn about their aggressive side. Often when boys are testing the limits of their aggression, someone wins and someone loses. To be healthy, a man must come to know and accept the experience both of winning and of losing. Young men use their aggression to find their place in the world. Often a teenager will need a series of these experiences to learn about healthy and unhealthy aggression. One day a man expressed his deep concern about teenage aggression today. He recalled that when he was a boy, if a dispute arose in his neighborhood, they would settle it with a fist fight. Now with the proliferation of firearms, teenagers are responding to conflicts with deadly force. The Red Knight energy is capturing these young men and the consequences are irreversible and deadly.

Wrestling with aggression is a necessary phase for men. It is both necessary and a phase. Some men never leave this phase of life and remain competitive and ruthless all their lives, which is to say, they remain stuck in their adolescence. We see this phenomenon acted out in business, politics, religion, and relationship. What often passes for authority, power, and strength is actually men overpowered by their own aggressive side, just as the force of the Red Knight's horse overpowered Parzival. When a man is overpowered by his aggressive nature, no maturing and good judgement based on higher values are possible. His world is therefore more chaotic, immature, and lacking in soul. In other words, he is living in the Waste Land. Unfortunately for him and the other people in his life, some men never learn how to find and use their aggressive side properly.

While some men act out their aggression, others fear it and attempt to deny it. These men avoid necessary conflicts and arguments that can bring growth and positive change. Because of their fear of their own aggression, they let themselves be dominated and controlled in their work, families, and relationships. Often this strategy of denial of the Red Knight leads to a man feeling impotent, depressed, and ineffective in his life. He remains dependent of someone or some group to define him and approve of him. However, his aggression does not disappear, it is expressive in a series of passive aggressive maneuvers that make it very difficult for others to know him and relate to him in a healthy manner—thereby he creates his own Waste Land.

For a boy to become a man, he must master his aggression. To be a man one must know aggression, and one must know how to control it. The challenge for a man is to learn the difference between healthy and unhealthy aggression; he must learn how to assert himself in his world and stand up and fight for his values without blindly controlling others with his immature power complex.

Finally, the image of Parzival putting on the Red Knight's armor over the Fool's Clothing represents another dilemma in every man. On the one hand, he wants to be a man who is self-sufficient and self-reliant—he wants to look adult and mature in his armor. On the other hand, he secretly wants someone else to be responsible for what is really his task—he wants someone to take care of him. Like Parzival, he does not want to take off the Fool's Clothing. How a man resolves this dilemma will go a long way in determining how much maturity he can achieve. For a man to learn to wear his Red Knight-armor responsibly and to learn to remove his Fool's Clothing are major challenges and tasks on the road toward maturity. Often we need help, guidance, and mentoring to complete this task. Parzival is about to experience the gift of such help.

The Red Knight's horse takes Parzival for a full day's ride until they come upon the castle of an old and skilled knight named **Gurnemanz**. Gurnemanz knows the Red Knight and thinks he is welcoming him into the castle. However, it is Parzival who greets him by saying, "My mother told me to accept advice from any man having grey hair. I will serve you for it since that is what my mother said."[2] When the pages take off Parzival's armor, Gurnemanz is surprised to see a young man wearing Fool's Clothing. Parzival's strong and beautiful body, a warrior's body, impresses Gurnemanz. As Parzival tells him the story of how he obtained the Red Knight's armor, Gurnemanz sees that he is a diamond in the rough—a strong adolescent who has the raw qualities to become a powerful knight. Gurnemanz also thinks to himself that this lad would make a fine match for his only daughter. Therefore, he offers lodging to Parzival. The servants attend to Parzival by cleaning the armor rust from his body and caring for the wound that he suffered at the hand of the Red Knight.

Gurnemanz, seeing Parzival's potential, offers to train him in the ways of knighthood. For two weeks Parzival stays at the castle where Gurnemanz trains him in the ways of chivalry, ethics, and the skills needed in battle. This beautiful part of the story shows Gurnemanz bringing out the potential of young Parzival. He teaches Parzival how to ride a horse and how to skillfully use a shield, a spear, and a sword. Parzival displays exceptional skills on the battle field and he dismounts five riders the first day. Besides the physical skills needed for battle, Gurnemanz teaches Parzival to honor the rules and the code of the knight. First, he tells Parzival that he must stop quoting his mother and that he must take off his Fool's Clothes. Parzival never wears the Fool's Clothes again, but as we will see, changing the inner attitude that the Fool's Clothes represent is far more difficult. Gurnemanz also tells Parzival that a knight must value women and that faithfulness and honesty with women are most important. Finally, he teaches Parzival that accomplished knights are always polite in society and do not ask unnecessary questions. Although it is the social convention of the time, this last piece of advice will not serve Parzival well when he arrives at the Grail Castle.

Gurnemanz's training of Parzival is an example of the experience of mentoring that is so helpful in a man's development. A mentor is someone who comes into a man's life, sees the potential in him, and encourages him to grow into himself—to develop the necessary life skills. It is indeed a blessing to have such a mentor, as he is often able to give a man what his father was not able to give. I have listened to many men tell their story of a mentor who helped them develop as a person or who influenced the direction in their life. I notice that these men always spoke of their mentors with a great deal of affection, thankfulness, and emotion. I have had several wonderful mentors during my life. One was the executive director of a social service agency where I interned as a college student. Mr. Henry took me under his wing, invited me to observe his interviewing and assessment style, exposed me to individual and group therapy, taught me about the criminal justice system and his value of helping the poor and mentally ill within that system, and he gave me challenging cases by which I could learn to develop my own people skills with his guidance. But most important, Mr. Henry showed me that a man could use his power, influence, and authority to help other people and to fight for values of justice, fairness and love. More than thirty years later, his influence and guidance remain as a powerful life-forming experience for me.

Many men remember their grandfathers as important mentors for them. A grandfather, if he himself has matured, has the closeness and the necessary distance to see the essence of his grandson. When a grandfather sees the deepest nature of his grandson and expresses his acceptance and pleasure in his grandson, that boy will feel greatly blessed and will naturally strive to develop and express himself. Time spent with a mature and loving grandfather helps a boy make the transition to young adulthood and manhood. By sharing his experience and his hard-earned wisdom, a grandfather can influence his grandson gradually and naturally to remove his Fool's Clothing.

During this mentoring period, Gurnemanz grows to love Parzival. His affection for Parzival is so deep that he takes him into his heart as his son. Gurnemanz had three sons, all of whom were killed in battle. In Parzival he has found the son for whom he longed. Likewise, in Gurnemanz Parzival finds the father that he always needed. As their affection grows, Gurnemanz offers his daughter **Laize** to Parzival for his wife. Parzival is infatuated with Laize and is awestruck by her beauty. However, something within him warns him not to accept Gurnemanz's offer. He refuses not because he does not want Laize, but because he is too untried and untested. Parzival has learned that a man must earn a woman's love. By this act we are seeing Parzival's noble character.

Though Laize does not become Parzival's wife, she is his first love. He has a crush on her and he experiences his first love-kiss with her. This scene describes a lovely experience for a man, that is, his first infatuation. It usually takes an experience of attraction to another to open a man to the world of the feminine inside himself. Falling in love awakens previously dormant parts of us. When we fall in love, we may take a new or renewed interest in poetry, music, and nature—we open to our more tender side. The challenge for a man is to keep this previously undeveloped side alive when he is not in his partner's presence. Falling in love is easy, but remaining open to one's feminine side is not so easy. For most men it is a lifelong task to remain open to his feminine nature even after the initial falling-in-love experience begins to fade. Parzival will take his experience with Laize forward to his next encounter with love.

However, at this time Parzival realizes that he must leave Gurnemanz and Laize to find his own adventure and his own way. Gurnemanz wants Parzival as his son and Parzival's heart wants to stay with Gurnemanz and Laize. Despite how sad it is for all of them, leaving is necessary for him. Parzival's inner knowing that he must leave is his higher Self calling him to his true path.

Parzival enters Gurnemanz's castle as a boy and leaves as a young man. This time he rides his horse with the reins slack. He has learned how to ride and control the horse. Now he eases up on the reins to let the horse take him to his next adventure. Joseph Campbell makes an important comment on this scene. He says that at the time of Wolfram the prevailing thinking was that the horse represented nature, the feminine, instinctive, intuitive impulse of a person, and that the rider represented the will, the rational side of a man. The Judeo-Christian tradition teaches that we must subdue nature, and that we should use the rational to control nature. It looked upon nature with suspicion, sometimes as the flesh opposing the Spirit. However, Wolfram is saying the opposite. By showing Parzival riding the horse with the reins slack, Wolfram advocates getting into relationship with nature, and then yielding to it. He wants his reader to see the wisdom God has place in nature and in human nature. He is suggesting that something bigger than the ego is directing our life, and that we can discover it in nature and in our own nature. Parzival leaves Gurnemanz with his reins slack on the horse; that suggests that he is learning to trust the wisdom of his feminine instincts. With this open attitude, Parzival takes the next steps that will take him deeper into his truest nature and his life path.

The Questions

1. What experiences have helped you integrate your Red Knight—your masculine aggression?

2. Are you able to control your temper and your rage? Do they defeat you? What has helped you to control your aggression and use it creatively?

3. Remember a time you took off on your horse and could not stop it (i.e., driven by an instinct). Describe your experience.

4. Look honestly. Do you still wear some Fool's Clothing under your masculine strength?

5. Who has been your Gurnemanz? Has there been someone, either male or female, who recognized you and mentored you? Write about these people and how they affected your life.

6. Remember your first crush—the awakening of your feminine side. Describe your internal response. What came alive in you? Can you see these qualities in your life today? Where?

7. Do you ever ride with the reins slack? Or must you always feel in control? Where could you experiment with letting go to something beyond yourself?

8. What are the images of violence and aggression in your dreams? How are you relating to them in the dream? Are you being portrayed as the aggressor in the dream? Write about this.

Chapter Four

Finding One's Love
Inner Life

Dreams contain many characters. Some are humans, while others are animals or inanimate objects. Let us look first at the human ones. The character that appears most often in my dreams is the dream ego — the "I" in my dream. Either I am deeply involved in the action of the dream or I am observing the action. The "I" in my dreams represents my conscious attitude about the particular issue that the dream is addressing. Remember the example of the lion dream. In that sequence the "I" in the dream is running from the lion. The dream is showing that I am afraid of this lion-like quality. Had the dream portrayed me as stroking the lion, as one would a dear pet, then I would be in a healthy and accepting relationship with my lion self. We can tell much about our current attitude by watching how we appear in our dreams and how we are relating to the other dream characters.

A second and very important dream character is the shadow. The shadow often appears in dreams as characters that are the same sex as the dreamer. In this context shadow refers to all those qualities that do not fit into our picture and definition of ourselves but are, nevertheless, part of us. We all have parts of ourselves that we had to repress to adjust to our family's expectations and to fit into our society. However, these denied qualities do not go away; they become the unconscious shadow. Most people who have a religious or moral upbringing see themselves as good, kind, loving, and fair people. Therefore, we banish to the unconscious qualities that are contrary to this image — qualities such as selfishness, violence, cheating, and irresponsibility. To have these shadow qualities is neither good nor bad; it is simply our nature to have them. Remember the magpie that has the white feathers of the dove and the black feathers of the raven. As Wolfram says, humans are part heaven and part hell. It is our task to come to terms with all the qualities in our psyche. These shadow characters in our dreams are trying to help us see and eventually accept the parts of ourselves that we pretend do not exist. What do we need to look at if we dream of a very mean man, a street bum, or a slick manipulator? What if Michael Douglas, Bill Clinton, Cuba Gooding, or George Bush appears in our dream? Each of these characters represents some part of our personality that the dream wants us to face and accept about ourselves. The shadow consists not only of the negative qualities of our personality, but also it contains all the positive and the superior qualities that are in us, but that we do not recognize. We call this aspect of the shadow the golden shadow. What if we dream of a very self-confident man, a creative artist, a strong leader, or a quiet monk? What if Ghandi, Jesus, or Nelson Mandela appears in my dream? Each of these characters represents an undeveloped side of our personality that the dream wants us to accept and integrate.

The shadow contains energy that we need for our wholeness. Without this shadow energy, we are one-sided and will unconsciously act out those qualities in our life. If we understand the idea of the shadow in dreams, and if we then seriously work with our shadow by trying to accept these qualities, we will be taking a significant step toward maturing and becoming a more authentic person. Let me give an example. More than twenty years ago I dreamed that I was in a boxing ring with a black man who was much bigger and stronger than I. The match began and much to my surprise, I knocked him out. However, I had a sick feeling that on the following day another match was scheduled and that I may not be so fortunate. As I worked with the dream, I came to see that the black man represented a side of me that was very physical and very earthy. He was dark because he was unknown to me. At the time of the dream I was living in a monastery as a celibate priest and I was using my intellect and my idealism to manage my way through life. The dream was trying to show me that the way I was living was too one-sided. I was in an unconscious battle with the physical and earthy side of my personality. In fact, I was trying to defeat it. This is not a good thing for a person to do. That black man carries a tremendous amount of energy, and I was trying to live without it. The warning at the end of the dream is also powerful; another match between us was already scheduled. I realized that if I did not begin to accept my physical and earthy nature, I would soon conflict with this part of myself. I began to look at situations in my life and instead of merely asking myself what I thought about the situation or how I was expected to respond, I began to ask how I really felt about the situation and what my gut response was. By asking these additional questions, I was making room for my instinctual shadow side instead of ignoring it. This dream challenged me to begin to get to know and accept the physical, earthy, nonintellectual side of myself and to give it expression in my life. The more that I considered this shadow side, the more rounded a person I became. I came to enjoy my big, strong, physical friend. I needed this earthy side of myself and the energy it brought me. Our shadow contains powerful energy that we need to embrace our life more effectively.

To work consciously and consistently with our shadow is to make a valuable contribution to our own growth, maturity, and well-being. Accepting our own shadow also makes a great difference to the people in our life. The more we can accept ourselves and our nature, the more compassion and tolerance we will naturally show toward other human beings. If a person does not accept his shadow qualities, he will be judgmental and rejecting of other people who have similar qualities. We cannot accept in others what we have not accepted in ourselves.

In addition, working on our shadow can make a positive difference in our larger society. Jung taught that each person's consciousness and choices affect the state of the whole society. In the following statement Dr. Jung is emphasizing that the man who wants to do good in the world must bear the burden of his shadow consciously:

> Such a man knows that whatever is wrong in the world is in himself, and if he only learns to deal with his own shadow he has done something real for the world. He has succeeded in shouldering at least an infinitesimal part of the gigantic, unsolved social problems of our day. These problems are mostly so difficult because they are poisoned by mutual projections. How can anyone see straight when he does not even see himself and the darkness he unconsciously carries with him in all his dealings.[1]

A third important character to appear in dreams is what Jung called the anima—the interior, feminine side of a man's psyche. The anima generally appears as female characters in a man's dreams. Often a man will complain about how confusing, complicated, and non-rational his wife is. What is amazing to discover is that a man's inner feminine can be just as complex, confusing, and non-rational as an outer-life woman can. Despite this complexity, a man's anima is very valuable for his health and well-being. The anima gives a man his sense of warmth, value, and contentment. She is the one who animates and inspires his life; without her life is sterile. As we have already seen, Sigune's demeanor represents Parzival's relationship to his inner feminine—to his anima.

How feminine figures appear in a man's dream and how he relates to them tell him much about his current state of happiness and his sense of well-being. A man's relationship to his anima will also greatly affect the quality of his relationship with his wife and other women. Like Keie, the ill-tempered knight, a man who is at odds with his anima will find his relationships with women full of conflict. Like all images in the unconscious the anima has two sides: soul enhancing and soul robbing. Imagine your feeling if the following images of the feminine appear in your dream: a joyful woman who is redecorating her house, a beautiful woman who is being tender with you, a loving mother who is caring for her child, or a sweet, innocent little girl. Now imagine the feeling you have if you dreamed these images: your aunt who is always critical of you, a retarded woman sitting alone in a corner, a raging madwoman, or a pouting, moody girl. All these images carry emotional energy. If you dream of any one of them, you are seeing an aspect of your own personality.

A man's anima is concerned with his emotional life. She values his emotional responses to life and wants him to express his emotion directly. Emotion is the psychic energy that occurs in our bodies when we have a meaningful experience. Some examples of emotions are joy, fondness, hurt, sorrow, fear, sadness, anger, and loneliness. Ethically, emotions are neutral. What we do with them and how we express them can be either creative or destructive. Although we all know that many emotions exist, many men struggle adequately to express the depth and breath of their emotions. Sadly, our culture socializes men to discount and repress many of their emotions. Consequently, many men allow themselves one emotion—anger. Anger is often expressed when a man is really scared, tired, hurt, embarrassed, or disappointed. We are very limited in our ability to differentiate and express the wide range of emotional experiences that we have every day. The feminine figures in our dreams are often trying to teach us to see and accept the rich depth and variety of emotions that make us human.

Another aspect of the anima is what Jung called the feeling function. The feeling function and the thinking function are different ways that we evaluate life's data and experiences. The thinking function evaluates life based on the principles of objectivity, clarity, reason, and logic. The thinking function has given a tremendous service to our society in the fields of medicine, technology, and science. On the other hand, the feeling function evaluates life from the criteria of relationship and human values. With the feeling function we decide whether something feels true or right. Our decision may not make logical sense, but we know that it is the right thing to do. When people are operating from the feeling function, we know it immediately because they bring a sense of warmth, presence, and grace to a human encounter. We feel valued simply by being with them. I know a man who brings his feeling function to his job as a manager in a small corporation. Although his staff sometimes fails to be efficient, he works with them and tries to understand why they are having a bad day. Though his boss would prefer that he fire some of his workers, he chooses to spend the extra time guiding and motivating them. This man is bringing an important value, the feeling function, into his work place. Often this quality embarrasses a man who is blessed with a strong feeling function and he will try to hide it, especially from other men. The feeling function is a wonderful quality and sorely needed in our world. Often the business world batters a man's feeling function; he learns to repress it and he feels inadequate because he is too soft. Therefore, in a culture that often overemphasizes logic and reason, a man's feeling function will make itself known in his dreams. He will dream of people, often women, who embody the qualities of the feeling function. His dreams come to help him see a side of his personality that he is neglecting.[2]

Another aspect of the feminine which is troublesome and common for men is the male mood. When a man is caught in a mood, he is possessed and held captive by his feminine nature. When a man ignores his feminine side, she then turns on him. The male mood is the poisonous atmosphere that seems to appear out of nowhere. Most men are very familiar with the experience of being in a mood. He does not know what caused the mood; all he knows is that nothing is right. He is irritable and eventually someone, usually his wife or his children, is going to be the object of his anger. He cannot seem to help this reaction. The male mood is an emotional possession. It is poisonous to us and to those we love. John Sanford, an Episcopal priest and Jungian analyst has a very helpful description of the male mood.[3] In describing a man's anima, Sanford uses the image of a woman who lives in the basement of every man's psyche. If the man relates to her, that is, feels his emotions—whether they are positive or negative—she lives happily in the basement. However, if he ignores her, that is, if he denies his emotions to himself and tries to stuff them through the trap door that leads to the basement, she becomes upset and angry with him. A man's anima hates being ignored. Instead of supporting his life and bringing contentment to him, she releases a poisonous fog up through the trap door. Consequently, the man is in a foul mood. He is suffering and eventually he may act out his suffering on those around him. The way out of the mood for a man is to relate to his feminine side, that is, to feel his authentic emotions. When you find yourself in a mood, if you can ask yourself this question: In the last day or two what has happened that either hurt or angered me? Maybe it was the way your boss treated you in a meeting, or perhaps it was something your partner did that you did not like but did not bother talking with her or him about it. If you can let yourself feel the emotion that the interaction created, the woman in the basement of your psyche will be pleased again. Thus, your mood will lift. Sometimes you may also have to discuss the situation with the offending party. If you are in a mood, the dream that night will try to help you see the emotions that you have been ignoring. You will dream of characters who are expressing your ignored emotions, like hurt, sadness, or anger. It is my experience that if a man can learn about his moods and learn the skill to get out of this possession, his interpersonal life improves dramatically. His dreams are trying to help him do that.

Now that we have examined the purpose of dream work and some common dream characters, in our next chapter we will present a method for exploring the rich meaning of dreams. For now begin to notice the different characters in your dreams, get a sense of their personalities and their qualities, and see them as symbols of an aspect of yourself that the dream wants you to be aware of and to integrate.

The Story and Commentary

From Gurnemanz' castle Parzival rides all day with the reins slack on the horse. He is wearing the Red Knight's armor without the Fool's Clothing under it. His mood is sad for he misses Laize. He rides a long distance that first day until he comes upon a well-defended city that is under siege. Parzival sees the evidence of many battles fought recently around the city. He leads his horse across a dangerous bridge and comes to the city gates. When Parzival knocks at the gate, a maiden in a window above asks him whether he comes as an enemy or a friend. She says that they do not need another enemy. Parzival tells her that he has come to offer his service. With that, the city gates are opened. As she leads Parzival through the city streets, he sees how the inhabitants are starving. It appears that they have not eaten a good meal in quite sometime.

The maiden takes Parzival to the city's young Queen, **Condwiramurs.** Her name means channel of love. She is a beautiful, radiant woman. Wolfram says that in her "God had not omitted any wish." She invites Parzival to sit with her. He is struck with her great beauty, while Condwiramurs wonders why a handsome knight has come to pay her a visit. It is an awkward moment, since each youth is fascinated by the other and is shy about speaking too rashly. Condwiramurs finally tires of waiting for him to speak and asks him from what place he has come. Parzival tells her about his time with Gurnemanz. Much to his surprise, Condwiramurs tells him that she knows Gurnemanz. He is her uncle and Laize was her childhood playmate. With that revelation Parzival feels a deep closeness to the Queen, as if she is family. Now they have much to talk about and they share an evening of conversation. Although the two youths share only a morsel of food, both are deeply satisfied by their time together. At evening's end, the servants lead Parzival to his bed for the night. It is a richly decorated bed, surrounded by candles.

Not long after he falls asleep, Condwiramurs steals into his bedroom. She kneels down beside his bed and begins to weep over the plight of her city. Parzival awakens and, finding the Queen kneeling at his bed, is startled. Since his mother told him to kneel before no one except God, he quickly invites her into his bed to talk. When Condwiramurs is assured that he will be honorable, she climbs into bed with him and tells him of her plight. Her city is under attack by an unwelcome suitor named **Clamidé**. He wanted to marry her, but she refused. In anger he attacked her city. In Clamidé's actions we see the difference between love and power over another. Power over another is attacking to get what we want through such behaviors as manipulating, lying, blaming, shaming, coercing, and using. Power over is the opposite of love. Condwiramurs tells Parzival that she will throw herself off the highest tower of the city rather than marry Clamidé. This thought horrifies Parzival and he tells her not to worry because he will take up her cause in the morning. Then Condwiramurs tells him this startling news: Clamidé had killed Gurnemanz's son to whom she was engaged. Parzival trembles at this news that the man who killed Gurnemanz's son now is attacking Condwiramurs. He feels angry and sad and he deepens his resolve to fight for the Queen. Parzival feels united to Condwiramurs through Gurnemanz and his family. After a lengthy discussion the two virgins sleep in each other's arms.

It was the custom of the time that one's chief officer do the fighting for his master. The next morning Parzival dons his armor and heads out of the city gates to meet Clamidé's officer on the battlefield. The battle is fierce. The spears of both men are splintered and their shields are pierced. Soon they are raining blows on each other's armor with their swords. As the battle continues, Parzival gains the upper hand and soon Clamidé's officer lay on his back with Parzival's knee on his chest and his sword drawn to his neck. Remembering Gurnemanz' admonition to offer mercy to one's enemies, Parzival does not inflict any more harm on his opponent. The officer surrenders and, in exchange for his life, Parzival orders him to travel to Arthur's court. Parzival tells the officer that there he will find a maiden who was struck on Parzival's account and that he must offer his service to her. The maiden is the Lady Cunneware who laughed for the first time when Parzival came to the court. Parzival also orders the officer to tell Arthur that the knight in the red armor sent him and that Parzival is in his service. The officer agrees and leaves immediately for Arthur's court, thankful to have his life.

That night two ships make their way to the city, and for the first time in months the inhabitants have enough food. Joy returns to the city that day. When Parzival arrives and takes up the cause of the Queen, the fortune of the city changes for the better. Unlike Clamidé, Parzival has pure intentions. He seeks no personal gain; he is motivated only by the desire to serve Condwiramurs and her people. The arrival of the ships with food is an outer manifestation of Parzival's generous and giving spirit.

When Condwiramurs learns of Parzival's victory and of the arrival of food for her people, she is overjoyed. Her affection for Parzival increases. For the second night she comes to Parzival's bed and again the two virgins lie together. They share their tenderness and warmth with each other; for the second night the Queen remains a maiden. Wolfram says of Parzival that he lies with such modesty that many women of his day would not have been satisfied. However, Condwiramurs is completely satisfied with Parzival. The next morning when they awake, Condwiramurs puts her hair up as a sign of her union with Parzival. They are betrothed to each other.

Meanwhile, Clamidé hears that Parzival has defeated his chief officer. Now he readies himself for battle. Parzival again dons the armor of the Red Knight and rides out to face the man who brought harm to Gurnemanz's son and to Condwiramurs' city. Again the battle is fierce. Both warriors are strong and skilled. Before long the combatants knock each other off their horses, and they continue the battle on foot—exchanging blows with their swords. As they fight Parzival gains strength, while Clamidé weakens, feeling as though rocks are pelting him. Eventually Clamidé is on his back with Parzival's knee on his chest and sword at his throat. He begs for mercy. Parzival orders him to ride to the castle of Gurnemanz and offer his service. Clamidé pleads with Parzival not to send him to Gurnemanz, since he has killed Gurnemanz' son and will not live a day there. Parzival tells him to go to Arthur's court instead and there he will find a woman who was struck on his account. Clamidé must offer his service to Lady Cunneware, tell Arthur that Parzival sent him, and that Parzival is in the King's service. Clamidé agrees and immediately departs for Arthur's court, thankful to have his life.

When the two warriors arrive swearing their service to Cunneware and reporting that the young fellow in the Red Knight's armor has defeated them, the whole company at Arthur's court is amazed. The Round Table pronounces Parzival worthy of the highest honor and judges Keie guilty of committing a serious wrong by slapping Lady Cunneware. The prophecy of the dwarf is being fulfilled; a wrong is being made right.

Condwiramurs thought of herself as the wife of Parzival even before he defeated Clamidé. She embraces him before her people and declares him to be her Lord and theirs. Thus, begins their peaceful and loving rein over this city. On the third night they consummate their love. Wolfram describes their union this way:

Two days and the third night they were happy with one another in their affection. To him there often came the thought of embracing her, as his mother had counseled him—and Gurnemanz too had explained to him that man and wife are one. And so they entwined arms and legs, if I may be allowed to tell you so, and he found the closeness sweet. The custom, old and ever new, dwelt with the two of them there, and they were glad and nowise sad.[4]

Sweetly Parzival and Condwiramurs renew the old custom and become one. Joseph Campbell emphasizes an important dynamic of their relationship. They married themselves. Though the Church and the clergy are always present in the background of this tale, Parzival and Condwiramurs marry themselves; they need no priest. Their relationship is one confirmed in love. The love itself is the sacrament. Their love is not motivated by lust nor fear (common reasons why people have sex), but by compassion and courage. Parzival showed compassion for Condwiramurs and courage by risking his life for her. Condwiramurs had the courage to withstand the advances of Clamidé whom she did not love. They did not bow to the pressure of power or social appearances. They knew in their hearts that their relationship was right. Their actions are a splendid example of using their feeling function.

For the next year and a half Parzival and Condwiramurs rule their people with love and they begin their family. One son is born and Condwiramurs is pregnant with the second son. In contrast to the other Grail stories where the hero is a celibate, Wolfram's hero is a married man and a father. Parzival's search for the Grail is the fulfillment of a full human life, instead of a denial of it. The religious teaching of the time emphasized that for a man to live a spiritual life he had to leave the world and live as a celibate. By presenting his Grail hero Parzival as a married man with children, Wolfram is saying that one does not have to leave the world to be a spiritual man. A full spiritual life is not opposed to marriage and family life. Wolfram is stating that the spiritual life blossoms in the ordinary human life.

This segment of the story shows the role of commitment as an essential element in a mature life. Parzival arrives at the castle of a queen in need. He offers to protect and defend her without expectation of reward or repayment. Commitment means working and giving oneself for the sake of another's needs. Living a life that puts other people's needs on an equal plane with one's own is a heroic act that brings forth a spirit of generosity, care, and joy. Commitment to another, a wife or a child, puts a man's life in a bigger context than his own and often provides a deep sense of meaning and purpose for him. Commitment and sacrifice for others are a significant way for man to remove his Fool's Clothing. No longer is he looking for someone to make his life better; he is offering his service to improve another's life. Paradoxically, the selfless act of commitment not only summons a man's responsible qualities, but also adds depth and purpose to his own life. Parzival's commitment to Condwiramurs and to their children gives him an arena in which to express and live the skills and values that Gurnemanz taught him. No longer the boy who left his mother's home, Parzival is becoming a man—he is removing his Fool's Clothing.

Parzival enjoys his life as a husband and father. Then one day he thinks that it is time to visit his mother Herzeloyde. He has no idea that she is dead. Unlike his father, he asks permission of his Queen to leave to see his mother. Condwiramurs cannot deny this request. It is a sad parting for the two lovers. Parzival leaves thinking that he is returning to his personal mother, but he is beginning a journey that will lead him to the Great Mother—to the experience of the Grail. However, Parzival has many miles to travel before he experiences the Grail. Most men's lives evolve in a similar way. The first half of their lives focus on establishing themselves in the world, usually through career and family. Often in their thirties something more begins to stir. From deep within comes a yearning for something more. If a man is wise enough, he will know that this is not a yearning for more of the same, but an invitation to open up to his deeper impulses—a inner push to search for that which will give his soul lasting meaning. Sometimes we do not even know that we are yearning for a deeper connection with our souls. We simply feel an inner restlessness. Parzival begins this significant phase of his journey with the reins slack on his horse. He trusts his intuitive, non-rational knowing to guide him.

His horse takes him many miles that day. Toward evening Parzival comes upon a lake where two men in a boat are fishing. He sees that one of the men is richly dressed and wears a peacock feather in his hat. Parzival asks if they know of any place nearby where he can spend the night. The man with the peacock feather in his hat is **Amfortas,** the Grail King. He is the wounded King, the King of the Waste Land.

Parzival will journey for several years before he hears the story of how the King became wounded. However, for the purpose of our work, we will hear the story now. In his youth Amfortas was a beautiful and gentle man who inherited his role as the Grail King from his father. The

Grail King is the guardian of the highest symbol of the spiritual life. Amfortas inherited this role, but he did not earn it. Inheriting a spiritual role in life is very different from earning it. We earn our spiritual life by wrestling with spiritual questions until we find the teachings and the way that bring life, passion, and meaning to us. When we inherit our spiritual role, we may go through the motions of a spiritual life automatically without ever truly making it our own. This is the state of many people in our society today—we inherit a set of spiritual principles without really examining their relevance to our lives. If we have not truly earned our spiritual life, an inner knowing may be missing. Then in times of trial when we truly need the help of a spiritual reality, the spiritual point of view and its guidance may not be accessible.[5] This is Amfortas' situation.

Let us now hear how Amfortas was wounded. One day in his youth, Amfortas rode out of the Grail Castle under the banner of Amor, that is, Love. However, the spiritual principle of Love is about to leave Amfortas—his spiritual life is about to fail him. As he rides past the forest, a pagan knight, a dark man from the Holy Land, rides out of the forest. Both men put their spears down and ride hard toward each other. Each man delivers a serious blow to the other. The spear of the Grail King pierces the pagan knight and kills him; the spear of the pagan knight hits the King in the pubic area and castrates him. Castration is the Grail King's wound and a mighty wound it is. Amfortas recovers enough to hobble back to the Castle where his servants attend to his wound. The servants discover that the tip of the pagan knight's lance has broken off and is in Amfortas' groin. The poison on the lance head seeps into his body. This poison will forever leave the King suffering intense pain. The servants use many types of herbs and tinctures to treat the wound; nothing helps the King's suffering. Surprisingly, the servants discover that the word Grail is engraved on the lance-head of the pagan knight.

That evening, on the Grail a message appears that states that the King's wound can only be healed when a noble knight comes to the castle, sees the King's wound, and with a heart of compassion asks the correct question. None of the members of the castle is allowed to help this knight; he must do this on his own. From that day on, the King remains in terrible pain. He could "neither stand, nor sit, nor lie down." The whole Kingdom suffers because the King suffers. They can only suffer and wait for deliverance.

What are we to make of this wound? When we talk about this section of the story in the men's group, I extinguish the black candle and leave the white candle burning. (Throughout the sessions a black candle and a white candle are lit on either side of a stone vessel that represents the Grail.) The extinguished black candle stands for the pagan knight whom Amfortas killed. The pagan knight represents our dark, unknown, rejected, shadow energy. When we deny our shadow qualities and figuratively kill them, we make ourselves spiritually impotent. Like Amfortas, we cut off our generative and creative powers. When we emphasize the white and cut off the black, we seriously wound ourselves. When we repress our shadow, our pagan knight-self, we experience these shadow qualities as foreign to us and as a threat. Literally, we will be in a battle with ourselves. Our sexuality and our aggression are two great forces in our psyche. If we repress these energies, they build up pressure inside us and, instead of making our life richer and stronger, they become destructive and control us. Joseph Campbell comments on the fact that the word Grail is engraved on the tip of the pagan knight's spear. His interpretation is that nature, as represented by the pagan knight, aspires to its own spiritual fulfillment. In contrast, Western Judeo-Christian thought teaches us to subdue nature, the body, and all its natural instincts. We have been shamed into repressing our natural feminine self and to fight against it. In other words, our tradition teaches us to kill our pagan knight-self. It instructs us that nature, which includes matter and the earthy side of ourselves, is contrary to spirit. Instead of teaching that the spiritual life is the completion and fulfillment of the natural life and that the natural life is the grounding and animating force of the spiritual life, our background teaches us to split ourselves. Because of this split we are severely wounded, like Amfortas.

Several years ago when my wife and I traveled to the rainforest of Belize, I witnessed one of the most powerful examples of Campbell's idea that nature seeks wholeness. One of our teachers in Belize was Dr. Rosita Arvigo who founded a center for the study and use of the medicinal properties of the rainforest plants. One day she showed us the poisonwood tree. If you touched its bark, you would have a severe skin reaction that would take many months to subside. However, if you took the bark from the gumbo-limbo tree, which always grows nearby, and rubbed it on the wound, the skin reaction would heal within the day. The gumbo-limbo tree is also helpful to reduce fevers or as a bath for skin conditions, burns, blisters, bites, rashes, measles, and infections. Additionally as a tea, it is helpful for kidney infections, stoppage of urine, and dropsy. Dr. Arvigo discovered one day that if she followed the roots of the gumbo-limbo tree, they always connect to the roots of the poisonwood tree. They have the same root sack. It is as if nature shows us that the gumbo-limbo tree with all its wonderful healing properties needs something from the poisonwood tree to make it effective. In fact, they need each other to stay alive—one cannot live without the other. The black and the white must be kept together and seen as two sides of the same energy. Nature and spirit must be kept together and experienced as two sides of the same energy. When our shadow energy is split from our spiritual values, the Grail King in us is wounded and the Waste Land is created. We, in the West, are people who have inherited a spirituality with a set of principles that are radically out of accord with the order of nature itself. Therefore, they are radically out of accord with our own nature.

Although Parzival does not yet realize it, he is meeting Amfortas, the wounded Grail King. Amfortas is now an old man who enjoys fishing because it helps him endure the pain of his wound. Parzival asks him for a place where he can spend the night. Amfortas tells Parzival that there is no dwelling within thirty miles, but that he can stay with him. He tells Parzival to follow a road with dangerous steep cliffs, turn right, and he will come to a moat surrounding a Castle. He is to ask the guard to let the drawbridge down. If the guard lets Parzival in, Amfortas will be his host this night. Parzival thanks the King in advance and heads up the road for the Castle.

Parzival has no idea that he is about to enter the Grail Castle. There he will have an experience that will change his life. What began as a journey to visit his mother Herzeloyde now becomes a journey into the depth of his soul and an encounter with the Great Mother. The adventure of developing his inner life has begun.

The Questions

1. Pick a shadow character from one of your dreams.
    -What qualities are in his personality?
    -Where have you seen yourself with these qualities?
    -What is its destructive potential?
    -What is its creative potential?
2. Describe a time you when expressed genuine emotion. What was that like for you?
3. Describe a time when you expressed a genuine feeling value? What was that like for you?
4. Describe your male mood. How do you feel when you are in it? How do you think others are affected by you when you are in it?
5. Look at yourself when you are in a committed relationship.
    -How are you at expressing genuine emotion?
    -How are you at expressing genuine feeling value?
    -How do you treat that person when you are caught in your mood?
6. When you are in a committed relationship, what do you think your partner experiences as your strength? What do you think your partner experiences as your weakness? Write about this.
7. The Grail King's wound is caused by his attempt to repress his shadow (his pagan knight-self). Do you have the same wound? If so,
    -How was it formed in you?
    -How has it controlled you?
    -Can you see how you have begun or could begin to heal it?

Chapter Five

The Grail Castle

Inner Life

Deciphering the message of a dream is an important task that takes effort. I have found that learning to understanding a dream is similar to the process of learning a foreign language—initially the process seems strange, but with some effort we learn the formulas and the new language begins to make sense.

One of the clearest and most practical methods for dream work is found in Robert Johnson's book *Inner Work*. The method, which is based on a Jungian approach to dream work, is a four-part process: making the associations, examining the dynamics of the dream, writing a sentence that describes the dream's message, and enacting a ritual to apply the meaning of the dream to one's outer life.[1]

A good way to learn Johnson's approach is to apply it to an example. I had the following dream about several years ago:

> I am in a building where I am pushing a disabled man in a wheelchair. We go past a guard who is standing at the entrance of an off-limits area. We greet each other in a friendly manner. Apparently we have known each other for a long time. Since I had never challenged him in the past, he is not very focused on his job of guarding the off-limits area. However, this day I wait for the right time and, while pushing the man in the wheelchair, I bolt past him into the off-limits area. I rush down a hallway until I come to a door. I throw open the door and discover a man who is lying on a bed and has been sleeping for a long time. By opening the door I wake him. We are both startled and I notice that he has a spot on the back of his head that has no hair.

When I awoke from the dream I wrote it down in my journal as clearly as I could remember it. In the next days I began to apply Johnson's method of dream work. The first step is making my associations with the images in the dream. In my journal I wrote a list of the major symbols or images in the dream: building, disabled man, wheelchair, off-limits area, guard, sleeping man, and head missing some hair. Then one at a time I listed my associations for each image. For instance, for the disabled man I listed: injured man, dependent man, limited man, and cannot stand on his own. For the man in the room I listed: awakened, groggy, Rip van Winkle, and becoming conscious. For the missing hair I listed: balding, aging man, and tonsure (the ritual shaving of the crown of the head to mark a monk or a priest). Then I examined each list of associations and discovered which association felt right for me. If I listen carefully to myself, usually one association will feel right; I will have a sensation in my body that tells me this is the right one for me. You may look at my list of associations and had it been your dream, you would have listed and chosen different associations than I. I chose "cannot stand on his own" for the man in the wheelchair, "becoming conscious" for the man in the bed, and "tonsure" for his missing hair. I did this process for all the images from the dream.

The second step of Johnson's method is examining the dynamics in the dream. To do so I ask questions about the people and situations in the dream and I examine how the dream characters relate to each other. Remember that how I appear in my dream represents my conscious attitude about the situation that the dream is addressing. The other characters in the dream represent parts of me of which I am not aware. I find the following questions helpful: What are the qualities of the individuals in the dream? How am I relating to them? How do these other characters relate to me and to each other? What are they doing and what am I doing in the dream? What am I feeling in the dream? The answers to these questions will begin to give me a sense of my conscious attitude toward the unconscious parts of me.

In my dream I notice that I am responsible for pushing the man who cannot stand on his own. I seem to accept this job. It is as if we move as one throughout the dream. I seem to have just accepted him as my companion in the dream. Since I am so familiar with the guard of the off-limits area and since I never before dared to enter that area, he has become so accustomed to my compliance that he does not see me as a threat. The guard works for whoever owns the building and is carrying out their orders. The rule is that no one goes into the off-limits area. Yet suddenly I disobey the order and, although I do not know what I am looking for, I run down the hallway with my disabled companion. There I discover the sleeping man who has some hair missing from his head. By examining the dynamics of the dream in this manner, I begin to get a sense of what the dream is trying to show me about me.

Noting the setting of the dream is also important. Where does the dream take place? Often the setting gives a clue about the issue that the dream is trying to address. It makes a difference if the dream takes place in a school, in a run-down home, in a huge mansion, on a lake, in a beautiful meadow, or on a speeding interstate. My dream takes place in a larger building, not an individual family home—more of an institutional setting. Therefore, it seems to me that the dream is addressing a collective issue in my life, such as how I relate to societal attitudes and values.

Dreams tell us a story and they follow a structure as any good story does. They have a setting for the action, then a statement of the problem, a response to the problem, and sometimes a resolution of the problem. This dream is addressing the effects of the collective thinking on me. The problem is that I have a masculine part of me that cannot stand on its own. Not only is that part of me disabled, but I am also limited because I must push him around in a wheelchair. A second problem is that there is another area within my psyche that for a long time I have felt unable to explore, because the building owners do not allow it. The guard holds the values of the building owners. For a long time my response to the problem has been compliance. However, today I decide to bolt and to go into a place in my psyche where I had previously felt unable to go. There I find a man who has been unconscious for a long time and is marked in a religious or spiritual way. The dream ends before coming to a complete resolution of the problem. Who is this man with the tonsure? What can I learn from him? Will he be glad that I woke him or will he be angry? Will the guard come after me and get me back in line? This dream highlights the principle that we dream about an issue only as far as we have lived it consciously. Therefore, it stops without resolution. It is my task to take the dream further and to finish it. We will see how to do that when we discuss the tool of active imagination later in this book. Nevertheless, I can work with this much of the dream now.

After examining the dynamics in the dream we come to the third step, which is writing a sentence or two that describes the dream's message for me. Doing the work of the first two steps before coming to the third step is very important. Many people make the mistake of attempting to interpret a dream without first listening to it and letting it tell them about itself—that is, without doing steps one and two. My preliminary interpretation reads like this: "I have an undeveloped masculine part of my psyche. I am breaking out of my socially prescribed restrictions and I am awakening an unconscious part of myself that has a spiritual marking." With this initial interpretation in mind, I begin to ask: What is this dream saying about me in my current life? Has anything happened recently that this dream is attempting to comment on? Where is this dynamic of my breaking out of restrictions operating in my life? These questions often help me see something that the dream wants me to be aware of about the way I am currently living my life. What attitudes have I been holding that have kept a masculine side of myself underdeveloped? How could I correct this problem? Can the tonsured man help me with this problem?

Finally, this third step has several additional rules. Avoid an interpretation that tells you something that you already know. Remember that the dream is always trying to expand your consciousness and will not spend its energy on things you already know. Avoid an interpretation that shifts responsibility for a problem onto someone else. For instance, my dreams will show me my part of the problem in my relationship with my wife. It will not show me where I am right and she is wrong. My wife's dreams will show her part of the problem to her. I can only work on my side; she will work on hers. Finally, live with the interpretation of a dream for a time and see if you can apply its meaning to your current life circumstances. Often the meaning of a dream will become clearer as we live with it. Sometimes a powerful dream will show us only one side of a dilemma and weeks later will show us the other side just as powerfully.

The fourth step in this process is to create a ritual in the physical world to honor the dream. This action begins to make the dream's message more alive in our waking life. The dream takes place in the nonphysical world. A ritual is an important step that helps the message and energy of the dream to become embodied, so that it makes a difference in our everyday life. It is so easy to forget that we have a body and that we live in time and space. The following are some examples of rituals that I have seen created over the years. A significant part of a man's dream was the image of a ball stuck in a fence, so he got a tennis ball and stuck it in the fence in his back yard to remind him of the dream's message. A woman who dreamed of a beautiful whale in the ocean went for a swim the next day and remembered her whale. Another woman's dream took place at night under a full moon. To honor the dream she found a picture of a full moon and hung it on her refrigerator. A man bought a package of cookies and re-enacted a scene in his dream in which cookies were used to cast a critical vote. For my dream I could have done several things: push a wheelchair around a building, find a picture of a man with a tonsure and display it in a prominent place for myself, or take a walk in a place that I would have previously avoided. I chose the final one and while I walked I thought about the ways my thinking has restricted my life and what I could do to change that. When creating a dream ritual, it is important that you do something with your body to honor the dream. By doing so, you will be making the message of your dream a part of your conscious, physical life.

More understanding emerged from this dream as I worked with it over the following weeks. Through active imagination work I discovered that the man whom I awoke was a spiritual teacher, and that he had many ideas that he wanted me to develop. Because of my work with this dream, I began to develop the idea of creating men's groups, in which I would use Parzival's search for the Grail as a metaphor to help men develop their inner life. I think my dream came to help me realize my deeper desire to teach, and to help men to connect with their spiritual source. This work had been off-limits for me because of my own self-restrictions. The dream challenged me to break through these restrictions and to express previously unused parts of myself. Dreams come to expand us and to help us live more of our authentic nature.

One final point about dream work is that we are the best interpreters of our dreams and the worst. We are the best interpreters, because we know our associations and which ones click for us. But also we are the worst interpreters, because we are dreaming about our blind spots — the parts of ourselves that are unconscious. Therefore, I recommend that you find someone whom you trust and with whom you can discuss your dreams to get his or her questions, comments, and perspectives. I have a trusted guide with whom I regularly discuss my dreams. He is an invaluable help for me.

Take a recent dream of yours, apply Johnson's method, and you will be amazed at what you discover.

❧

The Story and Commentary

Parzival leaves Amfortas, the old man with the peacock feather in his hat. He follows the Grail King's directions and rides up the steep cliff to the top, turns right, and there he comes upon a high and well-defended castle. The Grail Castle is so magnificent that it looks to Parzival as if someone has turned it on a lathe. Something is inviting and summoning about a castle high on the hill. Something in one's soul wants to reach for it—this is the soul's yearning for wholeness. When Parzival reaches the moat surrounding the castle, a squire from the tower above asks him what he wants. Parzival replies that the old fisherman has sent him and that he has already thanked him for his hospitality. Parzival comes with the correct attitude in which to enter the Grail Castle: one of gratitude and humility. These are also the qualities required to approach the unconscious. Parzival is about to enter the unconscious world—the Grail Castle. The squire lowers the drawbridge and Parzival enters.

He comes upon the courtyard that has beautiful grass undisturbed by war games. Parzival dismounts and walks his horse across the courtyard into the Castle area. Attendants greet him and lead him into the Castle. You will recall that the inhabitants of the Grail Castle are sorrowful because their King bears a serious wound. They do not show their sorrow to Parzival, but they politely take him into his chambers, help him remove his armor, and wash the rust from his face. They also give him a beautiful purple and gold robe to wear to dinner. They tell him it is the robe of the Bearer of the Grail, **Repanse de Schoye**. When the attendants take Parzival's armor to set it in a safe place, one of them, known for his wit, makes a joke about Parzival's joining the King for dinner. Parzival misunderstands the humor and becomes upset—clenching one of his fists so hard that blood squirts out of his fingernails and onto the beautiful robe. Like most of us when we are in an unfamiliar situation without our persona to rely on, Parzival feels vulnerable in this unknown Castle without his armor. He becomes threatened and defensive. Another attendant, who is attempting to reassure Parzival, tells him that the other man was simply making a joke and that he intended no harm. Parzival begins to relax. They tell him that Amfortas has arrived and that Parzival is to be the King's honored guest.

The attendants lead Parzival into the great hall of the Castle. When he enters the hall, he sees one hundred candles suspended above one hundred couches. Four hundred knights sit on the couches, four to a couch. A circular rug is placed before each couch. We cannot help but notice these symbols of wholeness in the great hall. One hundred is a complete and full number. Jung taught that in dreams the number four refers to wholeness or completion. He also observed that the circle or the mandala is the psyche's symbol for wholeness and completion. Symbols of wholeness adorn the great hall of the Grail Castle. These symbols suggest that Parzival has entered the place of the Self.

Once all the members of the Grail Castle are seated, the servants carry Amfortas in on a stretcher. Because of his wound, he can "neither stand, nor sit, nor lie down." Amfortas is placed before three huge fireplaces; he is always cold because of his wound. Although the fires do not eliminate the Grail King's suffering, they bring some comfort to him. Amfortas invites Parzival to sit next to him for the dinner. Parzival nervously joins Amfortas. When he does, the elaborate Grail Ceremony begins. A squire rushes into the hall holding a lance dripping with blood. All the knights in the hall begin to weep at the sight of the lance—the reminder of the King's wound. The sorrow that the members of the Grail Castle feel for their King overwhelms them. The squire takes the lance, circles the entire hall with it, and then quickly exits. Calm returns to the hall when the squire removes the lance. This occurrence stuns Parzival, and before he can recover, the doors at the back of the hall are flung open. Two beautiful maidens dressed in elaborate ceremonial robes process into the hall. They are carrying candlesticks. Then two more maidens enter carrying two ivory stools that they place before the King and Parzival. Next, eight elaborately dressed maidens process in. Four of them carry candles surround the other four maidens who carry a thinly-cut, transparent stone slab. This stone slab serves as the tabletop for the King when it is placed on the ivory stools. Two other maidens each carrying an extremely sharp, silver knife follow four more candle-bearing maidens. The knives are placed on the tabletop before Amfortas and Parzival. Six more maidens follow carrying glass vials of burning balsam that fills the hall with aromatic smoke and creates a sense of the sacred. Finally, the Grail Bearer, Repanse de Schoye, enters carrying the Grail on a beautiful, green pillow. As we discussed earlier, the Grail is the stone vessel brought to earth by the neutral angels. Wolfram describes the Grail as "the perfection of earthly paradise... which surpasses every earthly ideal."[2] Repanse de Schoye places the Grail in the center of the hall and then moves to the center of the circle, made by the other twenty-four maidens. The maidens form a sacred circle (mandala), a completely feminine one. By this Grail Ceremony, Wolfram is emphasizing the feminine nature of the Grail Castle. The Grail Castle, and likewise the unconscious, contains the fullness of the feminine life force. As a man examines his unconscious through dream work, he is exploring, accepting, and honoring the feminine side of his psyche.

When the Grail has been placed in the center of the hall, chamberlains bring golden bowls for each knight to wash his hands. The feast begins. The Grail provides each individual whatever he or she needs for nourishment—fruit, meat, hot or cold food. Participating in the Grail feast fills Parzival with amazement. Inside himself he begins to wonder about Amfortas' suffering and how it came about. However, he also recalls the advice that he received from Gurnemanz: knights do not ask unnecessary questions. This admonition was the social convention of the day.

When the meal is finished, a squire approaches the head table carrying a sword. He hands the sword to Amfortas who, in turn, offers it to Parzival as a gift. Amfortas states that he had used this sword in many lands before he was stricken by his wound. Parzival accepts the sword, but does not ask the questions that were in his heart. Seeing the King who is suffering so greatly should have prompted Parzival to ask the King the questions about his wound and about his suffering. However, out of fear of offending and out of adherence to social convention, Parzival remains quiet. He should have asked his questions: What ails you? What is the cause of your suffering? Why does this sword no longer help you? Parzival should have asked these questions not out of curiosity, but with compassion for the suffering King. In the Grail Castle we encounter ourselves. To see the wounded Grail King is to see one's own wounded self. Parzival does not understand this. If one is not moved with compassion for the suffering King, his heart is closed to himself and he is cut off from his soul.

Parzival remains silent. A moment of anticipation fills the hall. Recall that everyone in the Grail Castle knows the message that was written on the Grail the night of Amfortas' wounding: the King will be healed when a worthy knight comes to the Castle, and seeing the suffering King, asks the correct question. The critical moment has arrived and Parzival fails his task.

When it becomes obvious to all that Parzival will not ask the question, the recessional begins. Repanse de Schoye takes the Grail, bows to the King, and leaves the hall. The twenty-four maidens follow

SEARCH FOR THE GRAIL

her in reverse order. As Parzival watches the recessional, he catches sight of a beautiful, grey-haired man standing on the side of the Hall. This old man fascinates Parzival and he will only discover the old man's identity years later.

Servants then politely lead Parzival to his bedroom for the night. Four maidens attend to his needs and he falls fast asleep. Horrific dreams involving sword fights and battles fill his sleep. His body is drenched with sweat. These kinds of dreams come from the Self when we have missed a critical opportunity for growth and healing. Dreams like missing the boat, being unprepared for the test, or not knowing our lines for the play are often pointing to the anxiety the Self feels when we have missed an important opportunity in our life.

The next morning Parzival awakens to find the castle empty. On the floor lie his armor and his two swords: the one that he took from the Red Knight and the other that he received from the Grail King. He dresses, straps on his swords, and heads for the courtyard where he finds his horse saddled and ready to go. As Parzival rides out of the courtyard, he notices that horses have flattened the courtyard grass—the Castle is no longer a peaceful place. The drawbridge is down and Parzival rides across it. The bridge is drawn up just as he crosses. The drawbridge hits his horse on the hind feet, almost knocking Parzival to the ground. As he leaves, the squire in the tower yells at him, "from now on you will hate the sun, you are a goose. If you had only moved your jaws and asked your host the question! But you were not interested in winning great honor."[3] Parzival looks back for an explanation, but none comes. The words of the squire confuse him. Nevertheless, he follows the tracks of the horses from the Castle. Parzival thinks to himself that if he can find the Grail Knights and join them in battle, they will be happy to have such a great knight as himself in their company. Here we see the ego's ability to rationalize itself out of its anxiety and to delude itself. Parzival follows the tracks until they vanish. Thus it is with the unconscious world, it quickly fades when we return to ego, waking consciousness.

Parzival leaves the Grail Castle experience without healing the King and without gaining self-knowledge. However, self-knowledge is about to come to him. Awareness of his failure in the Grail Castle will come to Parzival from Sigune, the woman he met holding her beloved, dead knight in her lap. As we discussed earlier, Sigune is showing us Parzival's own connection to his true nature. Sigune is still holding her beloved on her lap—he is now embalmed. It has been several years since their first meeting and Parzival does not recognize Sigune at first sight. She is in a terrible condition. Her skin is pale and her hair has fallen out.

She asks him where he was last night. He says that he was in a noble castle about a mile away. She says that cannot be true since no dwelling is within thirty miles. However, she tells him that there is a Castle that only reveals itself when one does not seek it—the ego cannot make it appear. Sigune tells him that the Castle is named Mansalvasch and that in the Castle resides the Grail family. She tells him about the first Grail King, **Titurel**. Eventually, Titurel handed the role of Grail King to his son who in time handed the role to his son, Amfortas. Parzival does not know this yet, but these are his relatives. Sigune tells him that if he had been in the Castle he could have freed the King. Parzival tells her that he was there, that he saw the wonders, and that he saw the maidens.

Sigune recognizes Parzival by his voice and says, "Parzival, did you see the host?" Parzival asks her how she knows him. She tells him that it was she who first told him his name and that his mother is her aunt. Then Parzival recognizes Sigune and offers to help her bury her beloved. Sigune ignores Parzival's offer and focuses on what Parzival really needs. She points to the Grail Sword and asks if he knows its gift. She tells him that the sword will withstand the first blow, but then it will break. However, if he gathers the fragments and places them into the water of a certain spring, the sword will become whole again and stronger than before. Signue tells him that the water of this spring comes from the Source underneath the rock before the light of day shines on it. She then states that she is afraid he did not learn this secret in the Castle. She tells Parzival that if he did ask the question of the King, he is worthy of the highest honor. Parzival tells her that he did not ask any questions while in the Castle. Horrified at this, Sigune begins to weep. She cannot believe it. She tells Parzival that since he was there and saw it all, he should have felt compassion for the King and asked the cause of his suffering. She tells Parzival that though he lives, he is dead to happiness. Parzival still does not understand why Sigune is so upset with him for not asking the Grail King any questions about his suffering. Parzival asks her to be more friendly to him and states that he will atone for whatever he might have done wrong. She tells him to save his atonement because he lost his honor in the Castle. She, weeping more than ever, walks away from him. This conversation with Sigune leaves Parzival very confused. He now knows he should have asked the question of the King, but he does not appreciate the full implications of these events.

Parzival does not understand the meaning of his encounter with Sigune. Whenever he meets Sigune with her dead knight, he is seeing his own relationship to his soul. Symbolically, he is the dead man since he is out of touch with his true self. The soul does not really care what we have accomplished in the world and how many battles we have won. The soul only cares if we are alive to her, our true nature. Parzival is no longer the naive, young man who is simple and pure. He now has been put to a test of soul in the Grail Castle and has failed. He has made a mess of things. Eventually, he will discover that having this failure was necessary to learn the lessons that life is trying to teach him.

I have watched many people come to the moment of realization that they have been living the life they thought that they should live, based on their family's or society's agenda for them, instead of living their own authentic life. This is a terribly painful realization. To realize that one has spent years and made choices to please others and their expectations often fills one with grief for the lost opportunities. A sense of anger and betray accompanies this realization. One often sees that his unexpressed created energy has manifested in physical symptoms, anxiety, moodiness, or irritability. It takes courage to go forward from this realization and to correct one's course. Sigune gives Parzival and us some important guidance and direction when we come to this moment in our lives.

Sigune is not only confronting Parzival about his failure in the Grail Castle, but she is also attempting to teach Parzival a deep truth — a truth that every man must learn if he is going to fully mature. The deep truth is that every man, like Parzival, carries two swords. The first sword that Parzival took from the Red Knight is symbolic of a man's masculine energy that enables him to accomplish his goals and tasks in the outer world. The second sword, on which Sigune wants Parzival to focus, is the one he received from the Grail King. This second sword is symbolic of a man's ability to relate to the reality of the inner world and to gain self-knowledge there. By learning to use this second sword, a man gains his personal and spiritual authority. This second sword, the sword of the inner world, is the much-neglected sword. In the second half of a man's life, it becomes his task to learn how to use the sword of the inner world. By doing so, he will discover a new perspective about whom he is and how he is meant to live his life.

Sigune tells Parzival that the sword from the Grail King will break, but that he can learn to renew it in the waters from the Source under the rock where the sunlight does not shine. The inner world is the place of renewal. The water from the Source is the world of the unconscious realities — it is also where the Grail lives. If a man does not learn the secrets of the inner world and does not learn to renew himself there, he lacks spiritual power and authority. He is left with the broken fragments of his social and religious tradition. That is, he inherits a set of principles that will fail him in time of need. The purpose of dream work and inner work is to gain access to the Source that perpetually renews a man. My dream of the man in the wheel chair was showing me that my thinking and my compliance with a collective agenda were debilitating me and preventing me from expressing a significant part of myself that I believed to be off-limits. Whatever our current situation is, our dreams are trying to lead us to our true nature and to help us find a way to live harmoniously as the person we were created to be. Whatever our life situation is, we are called to find meaning, instead of wishing and trying to get a different life. We are being asked to find meaning in the life we have and to learn to celebrate it. To do this we need to learn to use our inner sword—to connect with the rich wisdom that lives within us. As Sigune tells Parzival, a Source is present within each of us that can help us with this task.

We now see Parzival confused and lost. Although this is a painful and difficult time for Parzival, it is a necessary stage for him to pass through on the way to wholeness. When we encounter our unconscious as Parzival does both in the Grail Castle and in Sigune, we are presented with a different view of ourselves than the one that our ego holds. We see our self from the Self's point of view. How we respond to this confrontation will determine whether we will live a life from our soul and its perspective or whether we will attempt to reinforce our self-image based on our ego desires and fears. The next segment of our tale will follow Parzival's struggle to make sense of his experiences in the Grail Castle.

The Questions

As we follow Parzival's journey, we are trying to get a clear picture of the wound that we are trying to heal. Question 3 asks you to review your response to the four previous sets of questions. Look at your answers to the questions about your father, mother, aggression, shadow issues, and your relationship to the feminine. As you review your answers, see if you can write a paragraph that describes your wound. If you can do this, you are seeing your destiny and the healing work you are called to do. Your dreams are trying to help you learn how to relate to these experiences correctly.

Question 4 asks you to do something right-brained. Instead of trying to figure out what to do with this wound, try this experiment. Sit in front of the paragraph you have written and take one of the mandalas provided and be with it by coloring it. Many men who have done this have had some interesting and powerful experiences by bringing the paragraph of their wound with the mandala—an image of their wholeness.

1.   Remember a time when you experienced a personal failure. How did you respond to this adversity? Did you learn anything about yourself?

2.   Do you have dreams of being unprepared for a test? Missing an appointment? Or a scheduled departure? If so, what attitudes in your life do you think the dream is challenging? What could you do to change this?

3.   Review the questions from Chapters 1 to 4 and your answers. What do they tell you about the nature of your wound? Write a paragraph describing your wound. (You are thereby meeting your wounded Grail King.)

4.   At least once in the next three weeks, sit before your description of your wound and color one of the mandalas provided. See where it takes you.

5.   Take one of your dreams (present or past) and work with it, using Robert Johnson's method:
     -Make associations with all the major symbols in the dream
     -Look at the dynamics, including the setting. How are you interacting with the characters and objects? How are they interacting with you? How do you feel in the dream?

-For the interpretation, write a sentence describing the theme of the dream. Ask yourself where this theme is operating in your life? What can you do about it?

-Create a ritual to honor the dream. Do the ritual and journal about this experience.

Mandala 1 by Sarah C. Cain

Mandala 2 by Sarah C. Cain

Mandala 3 by Sarah C. Cain

Chapter Six

The Confrontation
Inner Life

Ten of the men who took the initial course described in this book continued to work on their dreams by joining follow-up groups. The purpose of this second phase is to help men support each other in living healthier lives and to maintain a vital relationship with their inner life. Together they read books that discussed the challenges of being a conscious and healthy man, and they shared how they were applying the ideas from the books to their own lives. During each group meeting one of the men presented a dream using Robert Johnson's method. By sharing their dreams these men learned to challenge and support each other in the task of deepening their inner life. These groups have been a tremendous learning experience for all of us. They became a practical way for the men to develop their ability to use their second sword, the sword of the inner world. One of the men presented the following dream in the group. This dream is a good example of a man working with his shadow and learning to use its energy creatively.

David, a married man in his forties, dreamed:

I am in an office building with Castor Troy from the movie *Face Off*. Castor and I are suddenly on the same team—both of us have guns. I am thinking that he may have already killed people in the building. We both get on an elevator to go down, still carrying our guns. My gun begins leaking near the barrel. The elevator begins to stop at a floor and the light for that floor lights up. I watch Castor put his guns down the front of his pants (to hide them from the people who will be getting on). I start to do the same and then ask Castor if the guns could possibly go off in our pants. Castor smiles and says, "maybe" (Castor's personality and mannerisms are exactly as they are in the movie). I put my guns under my coat as people begin getting on the elevator, my guns continue to leak water. I move to a drain in the elevator floor so the water will funnel through the floor. The people who got on cannot see my guns but I sense they are suspicious of me because of the water leaking from under my coat. Everyone but Castor and I get off the elevator at a different floor. The elevator now moves up to the top of the building. I sense Castor and I cannot go back down on the elevator because people will be looking for us. Throughout the dream I am trying to convince Castor that I am with him and not against him. (I am not sure whether I am on his side or just trying to stay alive and not have him kill me). At the end of the dream my thoughts are about where I will put my guns at home so that they will be safe, but accessible if we are burglarized.

David made the following associations:

(The italicized words are the associations that clicked for him).
Elevator: up/down, small space, trapped, uncomfortable, *can't hide*.
Castor Troy: actor, cool, *sinister*; evil.
Guns: weapon, lethal, *aggression*, destruction.
Leaking guns: peeing my pants, fear, faulty, *gives me away*.

He noted the following dynamics in the dream:

-I am afraid of Castor and what he might do to me.
-Castor is exactly as he appears in the movie—cool, smooth, displaying a lack of concern for human life.
-People in the elevator are suspicious of Castor and me. They appear to want to get off the elevator fast.
-"Can't hide" association with elevator seems to make sense. My sinister side is eventually apparent.
-I don't want people to think that I am with Castor.
-Castor is comfortable with his sinister side, while I am not.

David wrote the following preliminary interpretation: "I have a sinister side of myself that is aggressive, while being cool and smooth. Others may be beginning to see it and I am afraid of getting caught." He then added: "I should accept my "dark" side and be more open to discussing it and not hide it. I spent much my life denying or covering up my dark side. I know shadow dreams have the purpose of expanding us. But why am I opposed to being with Castor? I was raised to believe that these qualities were wrong."

With the help of the group, David also began to explore where he may have been expressing his unconscious, aggressive, sinister side recently. How was this shadow quality showing itself in his work or in his relationship with his wife? The psychological reality is that what we are not conscious of will be expressed somewhere in our life without our awareness. David realized that the message he received from his family was to be very concerned about presenting a positive image to the world. He saw that this message conflicted with the shadow material that the dream was challenging him to face. Sometimes he felt ashamed and embarrassed to have an aggressive and sinister side.

During the next several weeks David worked consciously to become more comfortable with and accepting of his aggressive, sinister side. He began to see how he could use certain parts of this shadow to his benefit in tough business situations. He told the group that he would go into meetings and consciously bringing his Castor Troy-self with him. He reported that he became more effective in speaking his feelings directly, sticking to the point of a discussion, not allowing other people to manipulate his thoughts or feelings, and not worrying as much about how other people perceived him. David was happy about the changes he experienced because of accepting his shadow side.

For a ritual to honor the message of the dream, David took one of his business cards and above his name he printed Castor Troy. He then taped this card to his computer monitor, so he could see it every day. By creating this ritual David began to bring the energy of his dream into his concrete daily life. Instead of trying to be someone that he could never be, David began to accept this shadow side of himself.

As he continued to work with his shadow, David experienced a sense a relief. In addition, he allowed the other group members to see his shadow and found that they continued to like him and respect him even more. Support, encouragement, and acceptance from other men are great gifts that make the inner journey more possible. Though David could gain more insights from this dream, it was a very significant beginning for him. Four years later David continues to accept and integrate his shadow and he is a happier man for it. Ordinary men can have extraordinary experiences when they learn to work with their dreams.

The Story and Commentary

Parzival's life takes a significant turn the moment he fails to ask the question that would have healed the Grail King. He begins to retrace his earlier steps and he must now make good his past mistakes. Though he made mistakes unconsciously, Parzival still bears responsibility for them. Accepting responsibility for our conscious and our unconscious actions is not easy, but doing so is necessary for anyone who wishes to mature. Telling ourselves that we did not intend a certain outcome does not exempt us from looking honestly at the consequences of our actions. When we are unconscious, parts of ourselves are being expressed without going through our conscious, ethical values. Therefore, harm can be done unwittingly. Parzival begins to face the reality of his unconscious actions.

After leaving Sigune, Parzival rides alone pondering her chastisement for his failure at the Grail Castle. He soon comes upon a woman riding a miserable horse. Its ribs protrude and its mane is matted and untrimmed. The horse's eyes are sunken in their sockets and have the look of hunger. The woman on the horse is in an even worse condition. She too is starving. Half-naked she wears only a few rags, which have been torn in the briars. Her skin is sunburned wherever the rags do not cover. Her hair is matted down and she appears sorrowful. The woman on the horse is Jeshute—the first woman Parzival met in the tent. He took her ring and brooch and caused her disgrace. Her husband Orilus believed her to be unfaithful to him and since that day he has treated her with disdain.

Jeshute recognizes Parzival and begins to weep as she accuses him of being the source of her suffering. She tells him that if he had not come near her, her husband would never have so dishonored her. Parzival does not realize that the woman is Jeshute. He defends himself as an honorable man who would never dishonor a woman. (Parzival is blind to his unconscious shadow.) Jeshute ignores his ego-justification and continues to weep. Parzival then offers her the purple and gold robe that he received at the Grail Castle. Although Parzival is still unaware of his role in Jeshute's suffering, he displays a generous spirit. Jeshute, who certainly could use the robe as covering from the sun, strongly refuses his offer knowing that Orilus would be even more upset.

Parzival suddenly realizes that the sorrowful woman on the horse is the woman he met in the tent on the day he left his mother's home. However, before Parzival can say a word to her, Orilus, who has been riding some distance ahead, sees a stranger speaking to his wife. In a rage he pivots and begins to charge Parzival. The spear that Orilus carries once belonged to the Red Knight. The Red Knight's spear is now taking dead aim at Parzival. The helmet that Orilus wears was fashioned by the same smith who made the sword that Parzival received from Amfortas. As Orilus with a spear in hand and wearing a helmet linked to the Grail King charges Parzival, we see that Parzival's past mistakes are now confronting him. Parzival has made three unintentional and significant mistakes so far in his life. He killed the Red Knight, he contributed to Jeshute's being dishonored, and he failed to heal the Grail King. If a man has the courage to ask himself what role he played in creating the conflicts in his life, he will gain much consciousness and he will find an honest, healthy response to the situation. Orilus has his armor decorated with many images of dragons. When Parzival fights Orilus, he is fighting his own dragons—the mistakes of his past.

Parzival responds to the charge of Orilus. A fierce battle follows. Both men are strong and skilled warriors, but soon they are off their horses. As sword hits sword and as sword strikes helmet sparks fill the air. They deliver blows with such force that both men feel their knees buckle. Although Jeshute does not want either man to be hurt, she has to admire the battle between these two noble warriors. Eventually, Parzival crushes the dragon on Orilus's helmet. Parzival takes Orilus down onto the ground, places his knee on his chest, and he holds his sword over Orilus' throat. Orilus begs for mercy. Parzival orders him to forgive his wife. He refuses because he feels so wronged by her. Orilus tries to bargain with Parzival by offering him land from two countries. Orilus offers Parzival the land that he stole from Gahmuret. This means that Orilus offers Parzival his own land. Parzival has no interest in such a bargain, only in the surrender. Parzival continues to squeeze Orilus so hard that blood squirts out of his nose. He demands that Orilus go to Brittany, to Arthur's court. Parzival tells him that there he will find a woman who was struck on his account. He orders Orilus to offer his service to this maiden and to greet Arthur, telling him that Parzival is in his service. Orilus accepts Parzival's demands and agrees to reconcile with his wife.

Before Parzival lets Orilus go, he takes him along with Jeshute to a nearby hermit cave. There he finds an altar on which he swears an oath that Jeshute is innocent. He tells Orilus that when he first met Jeshute he was a fool, not a man. Parzival still has the ring that he took from Jeshute. He shows the ring to Orilus who now believes Parzival's unforced oath. Orilus places the ring on Jeshute's finger and reconciles with her. Parzival feels pleased because he has corrected his previous mistake. As Parzival leaves the two, he takes a multicolored spear that is leaning against the wall of the cave, because his was broken in the battle with Orilus.

Jeshute is thrilled to be relieved of her miserable position and to have her husband back. Orilus and Jeshute experience a beautiful reconciliation. Orilus apologizes to Jeshute for his terrible mistreatment of her. He takes his wife into her tent where she bathes and dons the robes of the queen—an honor she never deserved to lose. By admitting his role in Jeshute's dishonoring, Parzival is correcting one of his mistakes. To learn to correct one's past mistakes is a major step in taking off the Fool's Clothing. When a man can honestly look at his actions and admit his mistakes without rationalizations, justifications, or blaming others, he is overcoming his mother complex. Our actions, whether done consciously or unconsciously, are truly our responsibilities.

The next morning Orilus and Jeshute begin the journey to Arthur's court. As fate would have it, Arthur and his company have traveled to that part of the country where Orilus met Parzival in battle. The purpose of Arthur's journey is to find the young man who took the Red Knight's armor, because Arthur has decreed to make him a knight of the Round Table. Orilus and Jeshute soon come upon Arthur's camp. As ordered by Parzival, Orilus offers himself in service to Cunneware. He sees that she has the same dragon on her banner as he has on his armor. They soon discover that they are long lost brother and sister. They have a most beautiful reunion. Orilus tells her that the Red Knight has defeated him and that he has come to offer his service to avenge the beating that she endured. The knight Keie is becoming more dishonored with each knight who arrives to serve Cunneware. We also discover that Cunneware is the maiden who guards the well that can renew the Grail Sword.

The fact that Cunneware is the woman who guards the well that renews the Grail Sword is noteworthy. Some women, who have heard this story, have wondered aloud about why Parzival sends all the defeated knights back to Cunneware instead of sending them to his wife Condwiramurs. Cunneware, besides being a real character in the tale, also represents a part of Parzival's inner feminine—his anima. Wolfram tells us that she is the one who guards the well where Parzival can renew his own Grail Sword. When Parzival sends his defeated foes to serve

Cunneware, he is symbolically honoring his anima. When a man finds within himself, the well where his Grail Sword is made whole again, it means that he is learning to touch the eternally renewing waters of his unconscious and that he is gaining his own inner authority. He has a vital relationship with his inner world and he has learned to use his Grail Sword. Cunneware guards this inner well. An extremely important fact for a man who has a relationship with a woman is to know that he has to relate to two women: the human woman whom he loves and his own inner feminine. If he honors his inner woman by seriously developing his relationship with his inner world, the outer woman will thereby be honored and she will have a much deeper, more mature, and less petty man with whom to relate.

It snowed the night that Parzival rode away from Orilus and Jeshute; the snowfall was unusual because it was late spring. The snowfall signifies that Parzival is beginning a cold and difficult part of his journey. On the day of the snowfall Arthur's men had been out hunting and they lost a hunting falcon. The lost falcon spends the night in the forest; Parzival sleeps there too. Both the falcon and Parzival suffer the cold in the forest. However, Parzival suffers not only from the cold, he also suffers the harshness of his conscience for his failure at the Grail Castle.

In the morning the falcon pursues a flock of geese and wounds one of them. Three drops of blood from the goose fall on the fresh snow. You will recall that when Parzival left the Grail Castle, the squire called him a goose. Symbolically, Parzival is the wounded goose. When he sees the three drops of blood on the snow instead of realizing his mistake at the Grail Castle, Parzival imagines them to be his wife Condwiramurs. He remembers the first night he met her, when she wept as she told him of her plight. She had three tears on her face, one on each cheek and one on her chin. Suddenly Parzival is with her in fantasy. He remembers how much he misses her comfort. In his pain he longs for her warmth. Parzival's pain occurs not only because of his separation from his beloved, but also because of his separation from his own soul, from his true nature. This is a deep suffering. However, instead of experiencing his suffering, Parzival goes into a trance.

The trance, I have found, is an important experience for men to understand. A trance is an attempt to get out of and to avoid the pain of our lives. If we can find a fantasy, some compulsive activity, or some obsessional thought to take us out of our pain, then we will be better, we think. Of course, this type of avoidance does not take us out of our pain, but only takes us out of our real life. The trance gives us the illusion of comfort, but always leaves us empty. We are going into a trance when we reach for some substance or activity to numb us. These substances or activities can be alcohol, work, food, falling in love, TV, pornography, sex, fantasy, or sleep. It is a very important task for a man to recognize when he is in a trance and to learn how to get out of it. Our friend Parzival is caught in a trance and he will need help.

Parzival's trance consists of his sitting on his horse, staring at the three drops of blood on the snow, and reliving his first meeting with Condwiramurs. He has escaped into fantasy. Parzival does not realize that he is on the snowy meadow next to Arthur's camp. Arthur knows that his company has come to an area near the Grail Castle. He orders his knights not to fight so as not to do battle with a Grail Knight. That morning a squire looks out of the camp and he sees Parzival sitting in the snowfield with his multicolored spear raised. The raised spear is a signal that a knight is seeking battle; Parzival does not realize what he is doing while in a trance. The squire alerts one of Arthur's knights about the menacing knight on the snowfield. The knight convinces Arthur to let him go out to engage Parzival. He rides up to Parzival and insults him. Parzival continues in his trance and does not respond. The knight rides a short distance and then lowers his spear and charges Parzival. Fortunately, Parzival's horse turns toward the charging knight. Parzival, no longer able to see the drops of blood, temporarily comes out of his trance. He recovers his senses and delivers a mighty blow to the charging knight, knocking him off his horse. Parzival then turns his horse toward the three drops of blood and returns to trance.

Keie, the knight who beat Cunneware, sees what has happened and receives permission to confront Parzival. He rides up to Parzival, insults him, and slaps him on the side of the head. Parzival remains in his trance and ignores Keie's threats. Keie rides a short distance away, lowers his spear, and charges Parzival. Fortunately, Parzival's horse hears the noise and turns in the direction of the charging knight, by that averting Parzival's eyes from the drops of blood. Parzival regains his senses and throws Keie from his horse as it trips over a fallen branch and pins Keie under him, breaking Keie's right arm and left leg. Parzival turns toward the drops of blood and falls back into a trance. Men come and carry Keie back into Arthur's camp. The prophecy of the dwarf has come true; Keie does experience much sorrow at the hand of Parzival for his unjust and cruel treatment of Cunneware.

Gawain, who plays an important role in the rest of the tale, is among Arthur's company. He rides out to see what is happening on the snowfield. Gawain recognizes a man in a trance. Instead of challenging Parzival, he takes a silk cloth and places it over the three drops of blood. This action breaks Parzival's trance; he is no longer able to focus on the three drops of blood. Gawain's silk cloth represents the ability to overcome the trance. When a man learns to overcome his impulse to escape the pain of his life, he can avoid a trance. Parzival has something to learn from Gawain. If a man finds himself in a trance, he can begin to break out of it by asking himself the following question. If I were not using this substance or activity right now, what would I be feeling? If he can discover what emotion he is avoiding with the trance, he could face the emotion directly and he could discover what the emotion is telling him about his life. By doing so, he could make a more conscious and healthier choice about whatever is causing his suffering. I know a man whose trance consisted of fantasy with pornography. He used this activity to numb his loneliness and insecurity after a divorce. As he began to accept his pain, he realized that he was vulnerable to his pain before bedtime. Instead of giving into the impulse to go into a trance, he began a ritual of writing in his journal. Every night he recorded three things that had meaning for him: what he was thankful for that day, where he needed help from his Higher Power, and what he was proud of doing that day. Through this ritual he obtained in a healthy way what he was seeking through pornography, namely reassurance of his loveableness and a deeper connection to himself and to the Infinite. This man's ritual is a wonderful example of using Gawain's silk cloth.

When Gawain uses his silk cloth for Parzival, he returns to present time. Gawain then explains what has happened—that Parzival has defeated two knights, and that he has now avenged Keie for having struck Cunneware. Moreover, he tells him that Arthur and his company have traveled a great distance to find him and that Arthur intends to make him a knight of the Round Table. Parzival can hardly believe his ears. He is about to be made a knight of Arthur's Court! With joy, Parzival and Gawain ride back together to Arthur's camp. As we will see during the rest of the tale, Parzival and Gawain are united as brothers. They will become dear friends.

Parzival is welcomed into the court with honor. There he meets his former foes whom he sent to serve Cunneware: Clamidé, his lieutenant, and Orilus with Jeshute. Cunneware greets Parzival with a warm kiss and offers him her best robe. Arthur greets Parzival, praises his valor, and tells Parzival that he wishes to make him a knight of the Round Table. Queen Ginover offers Parzival a kiss and forgives him for causing her so much sorrow by killing Ither, the Red Knight. This is the first time Parzival realizes that the death of the Red Knight saddened others.

Arthur's attendants prepare a great feast during which Arthur will welcome Parzival as a knight of the Round Table. Parzival is elated to have accomplished what he believed to be his life's goal. However, becoming a knight of the Round Table is not Parzival's destiny. Parzival is about to be saved from his ego's ambition in a most unfriendly way.

A figure riding on a mule appears over the horizon. The mule wears a richly-embroidered harness and bridle; the mule is old and has split nostrils. A maiden sits on the mule. She wears a blue cloak and a fancy hat with a peacock feather in it. This is the same type of feather that the Grail King wears in his hat. Her hair is braided and hangs down onto the mule. Her hair is black, thick, and about as soft as pig bristles. Her nose resembles that of a dog and two tusk-like teeth protrude six inches out of her mouth. Her eyebrows are thick and braided and she has tied them with ribbons to her hair. Her ears are shaped like those of a bear. Her rough and hairy face does not exactly invite love poems. Her skin is the color of monkey skin. Her fingernails are like lion claws. She carries in her hand a whip with a ruby handle. The maiden on the mule is **Cundrie**, the messenger from the Grail Castle. She is known for her wisdom and is fluent in many languages.

Cundrie approaches Arthur and says, "What you have done has brought shame on you and on many a Briton. The best knights in all the land would be sitting here, if it were not now mixed with gall. The Round Table is ruined; falsity has joined your ranks...now that Sir Parzival has joined your company."[1] She chastises Arthur for calling Parzival the Red Knight, since the original Red Knight was noble. Then she approaches Parzival and says:

> "You are to blame that I have to deny the King a proper greeting...curse be on your beauty...you think me an unnatural monster, yet I am more natural and pleasing than you. Sir Parzival, why don't you speak now and tell me why you did not free the fisherman from his sorrows...He showed you his burden of grief, oh faithless guest. You should have taken pity on his distress...May your mouth be empty of the tongue within it, as your heart is empty of real feeling!...You are so shy of manly honor; so sick of knightly virtue that no physician can cure you...Your host gave you a sword of which you are not

worthy...Your silence earned you there the sin supreme. You death of joy and bestowal of grief."[2]

Then Cundrie tells Parzival that he has a half-brother named Feirefiz, the black and white son of Belacane. She praises Feirefiz by stating that he is an honor to his father, Gahmuret. Parzival is shocked to hear the news that his father had another son. Cundrie also tells Parzival what a great mother he had in Herzeloyde, and that because of his silence in the Grail Castle, he has failed her. Cundrie then begins to weep and tears stream down her cheeks. Of course, the words of Cundrie shock Arthur's court. Her fierce message humiliates Parzival. Before leaving, Cundrie issues a challenge to Arthur's knights. There is a castle that holds four queens and four hundred maidens captive. She wonders if any of them are man enough to free the captive women. After a parting goodbye to Arthur, Cundrie slowly and sadly rides away on her mule.

What are we to make of Cundrie? She is the messenger from the Grail Castle, that is, she is a messenger of the Self. As we discussed earlier, dreams have two points of view: that of the ego and that of the Self. Parzival wants to be a knight of the Round Table; this is his ego ambition. His destiny is to do the work of healing the Grail King; this is the point of view of the Self. When we turn away from the Self, even if it is for a worthy cause, the unconscious unleashes a powerful force—in this case Cundrie—because the Self wants to get us back on our true path. The dreams and messages from our unconscious will appear hostile and attacking to our ego, when we are disconnected from our soul's purpose. Cundrie is angry and ugly. She comes to destroy Parzival's misguided ambition. She carries the energy of the East Indian goddess Kali, who is the goddess of death and renewal. Kali kills what is foul and needs to die for the sake of new life. She kills not for the sake of killing, but for the sake of life. We see this energy in Jesus when he cleared the temple or in the Twelve Step work of tough love.

Parzival's mistake is not some bad or evil deed, but unconsciousness. Parzival failed to express compassion to the wounded King because he wanted to follow the prescribed way—society's definition of a proper knight. His misguided and inauthentic attitude draws Cundrie to him. Cundrie energy is a powerful aspect of the divine feminine that appears horrible and ugly when we are off our path. She is not a pretty sight. Yet she is necessary because she holds our feet to the fire of transformation. Cundrie wounds Parzival's ego because his view of himself is too narrow to fully contain his true nature and destiny. Cundrie brings a necessary wounding that is meant to open Parzival by first cracking his ego ambition.

I had a dream more than twenty years ago, when I was in an immense inner conflict about which path I was to follow—whether to stay in a monastic community or leave to live a married life. In the dream I was driving down a road toward the city where I was living. Suddenly, the car veered off the road into the ditch and burned to ashes with me in it. This dream terrified me. For weeks I dreaded driving past the spot on the road that I saw in the dream. I feared that the dream might be a premonition of my death. However, I eventually came to see the symbolic meaning of the dream. The dream confronted me with a Cundrie-like force that wanted to stop me from going back to life that I knew. My desire to hold onto my life and my fear of the future were blocking the movement of the Self. Fortunately, I eventually understood the message of the dream, made the necessary changes, and took that same road out of town to an uncertain future. I never looked back.

As Cundrie rides away she passes a knight, who is approaching Arthur's camp. The knight enters Arthur's camp, finds Gawain, and falsely accuses him of killing his lord. The knight challenges Gawain to a battle in forty days to avenge the death of his lord. Because Arthur's court does not know that the accusation against Gawain is false, Gawain's name is tarnished until he can prove himself innocent. Gawain joins Parzival by being dishonored before Arthur's court. They are now both shamed. By this circumstance Wolfram is linking Parzival and Gawain. As we will see in the following chapters, Gawain and Parzival will be showing us the two paths for self-knowledge — the outer and the inner way.

As they are readying themselves to leave Arthur's Court, Gawain gives Parzival a parting wish. He says, "God be with you." Parzival, still stunned and confused by the events of the past days says, "What is God?" He tells Gawain that he served God the best he could and now he is disgraced. His religious container can no longer hold him; the belief system of his childhood has shattered. Parzival exclaims that he no longer believes in God. With this statement Parzival begins a long period of doubt. Doubt is a period in a person's life that the spiritual writers call the "dark night of the soul." Doubt is a time of being lost, alone, and disoriented about how to live our life. The way we have been living is no longer acceptable to us, but we have not yet discovered a new, healthier way to live. During a period of doubt we often feel a great deal of anxiety, because our life seems so out of control. To come to the Grail one must experience this time of re-evaluating and redefining the values in our life. Doubt is a necessary time of transformation, but it is a painful one. Parzival leaves Arthur's camp alone to begin his period of doubt.

The Questions

1. Remember a time you had to go back and correct something that you had done wrong. How was that for you? What did you learn?

2. How are you at making amends—graceful or reluctant? Are there situations in your life where amends are still needed from you? If so, are you willing to face these?

3. Do you go into a trance? What trance substances or activities do you choose? Can you see what pain you are trying to avoid by this? How are you at using "Gawain's silk cloth"—are you able to get yourself out of trance behavior?

4. Has anyone ever been Cundrie for you, i.e., confronted you strongly about how you were deceiving yourself consciously or unconsciously? What was that like for you?

5. Have you ever been Cundrie for someone else? If so, what was that like for you?

6. Take another dream and work with it according to Robert Johnson's method:
   associations, dynamics, interpretation, and ritual.

Chapter 7

Through Doubt to Breakthrough
Inner Life

Peter is a member of my ongoing group that focuses on supporting and encouraging men to maintain a healthy inner life. He is a 52-year-old college professor and a social activist. When he first entered therapy, he was quite skeptical about the existence or value of an inner life, but over the years he has developed a deep appreciation and respect for his inner world. Peter presented the following dream to the group:

> My father, his father (my grandfather, Harry), and I have been taken to a restaurant by a group of women. It is a ceremony of some sort, a combination of celebration and a marking of death. The scene shifts to a cemetery and only the men are there. I realize that this is about death. An evil spirit emerges from the ground, from a grave site. It is small, translucent, and energetic—like a swirling fish-fillet or the created image in *Ghostbusters*. It has great energy and it hurls itself up from the ground at me. I keep throwing it back to the ground. I know we cannot get on to why we are here until this force has been overcome. I keep throwing it to the ground and it keeps rising back up. I realize that I must say a Jewish prayer "Baruch atah adonai…" As I finish the prayer and throw it down one more time, it dissolves into the ground. It is finished. Now we can proceed. My father says: "It is a hard thing for a father to bury his son."

Peter then made the following associations:

Father and grandfather: the male side of the family, my
masculinity.
Women: my feminine side, feeling function.
Restaurant: a place to eat, be fed, celebrate, enjoy.
Cemetery: death, peacefulness, connection with generations
gone by, spirituality.
Evil spirit: pure energy, threatening me, a source of fear.
Jewish prayer: spirituality and ritual words said by others, a
way of being connected.

He noted the following dynamics in the dream: "I had fear in the
beginning. I wondered if it concerned my death. I had fear of the evil
spirit and a determination to defeat it. There was a sense of solemnity
and grief. I had tremendous energy trying to stand up to the evil spirit.
I also am listening to my father's words at the end of the dream."

This dream is a wonderful illustration of the fact that one cannot
merely read a book of dream symbols to learn the meaning of a dream.
One has to put the dream into the context of the life and history of
the dreamer. When Peter began to discuss with the group, his dream
and his associations, more of the meaning began to unfold for him. He
described the characteristics of his father and grandfather as men with
much energy, never taking a quiet moment, and always trying to make
things happen to avoid emotions. Peter began to see that the dream
was asking him to examine the role model that his male ancestors gave
him. Does he relate to life like his father and grandfather did? Has he
developed a different style?

I pointed out that the dream does not tell anything about the "evil
spirit," except that it is threatening to Peter. Often something appears
evil or dangerous to the dream-ego because it is something we have
not yet faced or we are afraid to face. Before he can fully understand
the dream, Peter must determine what this spirit is. Some members of
the group thought it was interesting that Peter turned to a traditional
Jewish prayer (his childhood roots) for assistance. When asked what
his reaction was to his father's closing statement about how difficult
burying his son is for a father, a memory surprised Peter. He recalled
that sixteen years earlier his grandfather Harry had in fact buried his
son Marshall (Peter's uncle). Peter trembled as he recalled how he was
once close to his uncle Marshall. When our body responds as Peter's
did, we know that it is confirming the truth of what is being said. Peter
then acknowledged that he had the same reaction to Marshall as he
had to all the men in his family. He was both attracted to Marshall

and repulsed by his excessively active lifestyle and his need to be the center of attention. Marshall was also a college professor in the same field of study as Peter's. Peter realized how much they had in common. Then Peter reported that he had not attended Marshall's funeral. He saw his decision not to attend his uncle's funeral as his unconscious continuation of his family's emotional style—avoid emotional contact and go through life with a stoic attitude.

From his associations and from the insights he discovered while discussing this dream in the group, Peter wrote the following beginning interpretation: "I need to reconnect with my Uncle Marshall. I was close to him at some point, but did not attend his funeral. I never really acknowledged his contributions to me. I never said goodbye."

This dream continues to be meaningful to Peter on many levels. His dream left him with the following questions: Who is this spirit? Why must I wrestle with it? How is this connected to my spirituality? Was Uncle Marshall a like-spirit to me? Other questions came from the group discussion: Could this dream also be commenting on the grief that Peter may be feeling concerning the son he never had? What role do the women in the dream play and what might they have to tell him about this situation?

Peter continued to reflect on the meaning of his dream for several years. The dream raised many other issues for him. It challenged him to look at his image of himself as a man and to examine his ambivalent feelings about the men in his family. Previously Peter shared with the group a series of dreams in which he found himself with men whom he did not respect or whose lifestyles were very different from his own. Peter realized that his unconscious was asking him to examine the way he viewed men and how he related to them.

Finally, Peter's dream continues to challenge him to examine his view of his spirituality and especially Judaism, which he moved away from years ago. Peter believes that without the questions, responses, and support of the group he would have had a very difficult time realizing the various dimensions of his life that this dream wanted him to examine.

For his ritual to honor this dream Peter intends to obtain a copy of his uncle Marshall's dissertation and to spend the day reading it in a nearby Jewish cemetery. By that, he hopes to deepen the meaning of his dream and to reconnect with the spirit of his uncle.

Many of our dreams comment on the events of the last day or two of our lives. Occasionally we will, like Peter, have a big dream. A big dream is a dream that is trying to help us with the bigger issues in our lives. This dream challenged him to examine his image of himself as a man, his style of relating to men, his spirituality, and his feelings about death. Peter will continue to work with this dream for many months and maybe years, as he attempts to understand the depth of its message.

Dreams are gateways to the hidden and unknown parts of us. Ordinary men like David and Peter can learn to unlock the mystery of the dream world and gain much insight into themselves. Through dream work we can become more aware of our shadow energies and our unused potential, so that we can bring more of these qualities to our waking life. The more we know about ourselves, the more options and choices we will have in our daily dealings with others. By their dream work David and Peter are displaying how a man can develop the skill of using his second sword—his power and authority in the inner world.

The Story and Commentary

When we last left Parzival, he was still stinging from Cundrie's harsh words. Parzival and Gawain, who was also dishonored before Arthur's court, are preparing to leave. Yet before they do, Parzival addresses another matter. Clamidé, the previously unwelcome suitor of Condwiramurs, now has become quite fond of Cunneware. He asks Parzival to talk to Cunneware for him. When Parzival tells Lady Cunneware about Clamidé's affection for her, she is flattered and acknowledges her fondness for Clamidé. Because she and Clamidé begin a love relationship, Parzival is freed from being her protector. For the rest of the tale whenever Parzival defeats a knight in battle, he sends the knight back to his wife Condwiramurs to offer his service to her.

As Parzival prepares to leave, several people from Arthur's court offer him comfort and a kind farewell. A woman from the Middle East is among them. She recalls for Parzival that Cundrie named Feirefiz his brother. She tells Parzival that she knows Feirefiz, that his power extends widely, and that the people of the Middle East respect and worship Feirefiz as a god. The woman then describes Feirefiz as strong, handsome, and with skin that has a wonderful sheen because it is both black and white. She says that Feirefiz is a skilled knight and that in a joust with Feirefiz, no man has ever remained seated on his horse. Finally, she tells Parzival that Feirefiz is known for his generosity. Parzival is so surprised to discover that he has a brother that he remains speechless about this news. The woman then leaves Parzival with words of praise. Parzival thanks the woman for her kindness, but he tells her that her words give him no comfort. He says:

> I cannot cast off my sorrow, and I shall tell you why. I can find no words for the suffering as I feel it within me when many a one, not understanding my grief, torments me, and I must then endure his scorn as well. I will allow myself no joy until I have seen the Grail, be the time short or long. My thoughts drive me toward that goal, and never will I swerve from it as long as I shall live. If I am to hear the scorn of the world because I obeyed the law of courtesy, then his counsel may not have been wholly wise. It was the noble Gurnemanz who

advised me to refrain from impertinent questions and resist
all unseemly behavior.[1]

With this oath Parzival says goodbye to Arthur and Cunneware.
Gawain turns to Parzival and says, "God guide you on your way." Parzival
replies, "What is God?" You will recall that the first time Parzival asked
this question, it was addressed to his mother. Then Parzival was an
innocent boy who was curious about his mother's beliefs. However, the
question now bears the heaviness of his sorrow. He is confused about
what has happened to him. He thought he was doing the right thing
by not asking any unnecessary questions in the Grail Castle. Now he
discovers from Cundrie that he made a significant mistake. Therefore,
he says to Gawain:

> If He were mighty, if God could rule with power, He would
> never have imposed such disgrace on us both. I was in his
> service since I hoped to receive his grace. But now I shall
> renounce His service, and if He hates me, that hate I will
> bear.[2]

With this statement Parzival begins his long period of doubt.
He began his life, as we all do, in a period of innocence; a time of
unquestioning acceptance of what others told him. Now however,
Parzival's period of doubt has arrived. For Parzival doubt is a time of
reexamining much of what his society taught him. Parzival's image
of God no longer gives him comfort and meaning. For him, God is
dead. All his outer symbols, images, and doctrine now fail to mediate
an experience of the Divine for him. It is a time of confusion and
disorientation. Although doubt is a painful stage of life, it is also the
necessary stage during which Parzival must sort out what is true for him.
In doing so, he may arrive at a new understanding and relationship with
the Divine. Only by enduring this time of disintegration will Parzival
come to know the reality of the god within. Having the courage to
wrestle with and endure a period of doubt is another important step for
any man who wants to remove his Fool's Clothing and wants to take full
responsibility for the values that guide his life. We are greatly tempted
to avoid this period of our life by retreating into comfortable societal
roles and socially acceptable opinions. By doing so, we abort the life the
Self wants for us. Most people, whom the Self hurls into their period
of doubt, find themselves outside the collective and societal attitudes
that once dictated their life. For the period of doubt to be a positive and

life-giving experience we must learn how to wait in the darkness until the new light comes. Fortunately, Parzival finds the courage to face and endure this difficult time.

Parzival leaves Gawain with a final thought, "Friend, when it comes your time to fight, may a woman be your shield in battle and may she guide your hand." Parzival has learned to trust a woman's love. He trusts his experience. Although Parzival doubts the supernatural, he relies on what is natural and real—a woman's love. Parzival leaves Arthur's court no longer wearing the armor of the Red Knight. He wears silver armor and leaves his Red Knight period behind. The sword of the Red Knight—his masculine power of goals, order, competition, and will power in matters of the outer life—cannot help him out of his current difficulty. The period of doubt is a struggle of the inner life. Parzival leaves Arthur's court with remorse, sadness, and doubt. Confused about how to live his life, Parzival vanishes from the story for a time and Gawain takes a center stage in the tale. Parzival and Gawain represent two parts of human nature: Parzival, the inner way to self-knowledge and Gawain, the outer way. To get to the Grail, we need both of them. In the next chapter we will follow Gawain's way—self-knowledge through relationship.

Parzival's period of doubt lasts for more than four arduous years. We do not know exactly what Parzival does during this time, but Wolfram tells us that he had many adventures "on horseback and in ships on the sea." During this entire time, Parzival continues his search for the Grail. Wolfram tells us that he has learned to renew the Grail Sword that he received from Amfortas. The Grail Sword, we are told, did break once and Parzival took the pieces to a spring that flowed from under a rock and in those waters the Sword became whole again. This image of the renewal of the Grail Sword shows us that Parzival has been learning the skills and the power of the inner life. When we are in the period of doubt, although we feel lost, aimless, and have low energy, we can learn much about our self by paying attention to the messages from the inner world. If we approach the period of doubt correctly, it can be a time of significant personal transformation. When we are in our period of doubt, we discover that the way we have been living our life no longer gives us meaning and that nothing has yet emerged to replace it. We must embrace and endure this experience. The temptation is to replace this period with something else—to try to get a new life. However, that approach would only abort our transformation. If we can endure this process, it will release us when it has sufficiently changed us. I remember Robert Johnson saying that when life gets the darkest, when we are sure we cannot endure it another moment, just wait ten more minutes because the situation is about to transform. If we can endure this period with courage and continue to seek our truth, we will learn quite a bit about how to renew our Grail Sword—we will gain our personal authority from the inside. Parzival chooses to continue to seek the Grail and to embrace his period of doubt for four long years.

When Parzival reemerges in the story he is riding in a forest and he comes upon a hermitage. Since no one has made a path to it, he must ride over some fallen trees. As he comes near the hermitage he asks if anyone is inside. Much to his surprise, a woman responds. He dismounts, removes his sword, and approaches the hermitage on foot. He looks in and sees a woman kneeling in prayer. She wears the headband of a widow and on her finger she wears a ring. The woman is Sigune. She has buried her beloved knight under the floor of her hermitage. She stays with him in sorrow and in prayer. At first neither of the cousins recognizes the other. Sigune asks Parzival to sit on the bench outside the window while she sits on the chair inside. They begin to talk. Parzival asks how she could survive so deep in the forest with no path leading in or out. Sigune tells him that her food comes directly from the Grail Castle. Every Saturday night Cundrie the Grail Messenger brings food to her for the week. Parzival thinks that she is trying to mislead him. Therefore, he teases her about the ring she is wearing by saying that he thought that a hermit was not supposed to have a love relationship. Sigune then tells him that she wears the ring in honor of her beloved man whom Orilus killed. She says that although she is in deep sorrow, she does not feel alone. She faithfully remains present at her beloved's tomb. Sigune tells Parzival that her beloved is the other half of herself. With this conversation Parzival recognizes the woman as his cousin, Sigune. He takes off his head covering and she recognizes him. Sigune asks Parzival about his search for the Grail. Has he discovered its true nature? How has his journey gone? Parzival responds by pouring out his grief to her. He tells her that he has lost the Grail, and that he has been searching for it ever since the day they last spoke. He shares with her that his heart aches over the fact that for all this time he has also been separated from his beloved wife. He asks for her help. For the first time Parzival can identify with Sigune. Both grieve their losses; Parzival grieves the loss of the Grail and his wife, while Sigune grieves the loss of her beloved. Parzival no longer regresses into a trance. He faces his sorrow and opens his heart to Sigune. In response to Parzival's vulnerability, Sigune now expresses sorrow for him, instead of her previous censures. Then she tells him that Cundrie's tracks are still fresh, and she suggests that he can probably follow them back to the Grail Castle.

We see an important dynamic for men in this part of Parzival's journey. For Parzival to learn about his own soul, he has to be separated from his wife Condwiramurs. The journey into the inner life is a solitary one. When a man is called to develop his relationship with his inner world, he often finds himself separated from his partner. Depending on the feminine energy of his partner to care for the needs of his inner life is sometimes too easy for a man. Initially we need another to awaken us to our inner world. However, in time, life will bring us the experience of separation from our partner to create the space necessary for us to go within. I do not necessarily mean physical, legal separation, although in extreme situations it does come to that. Life will provide opportunities for a man to turn within instead of depending on his wife or partner for an experience of his own inner life. For instance when children arrive, the dynamics of his marriage change significantly, because his wife is now also focused on her role as mother. When her career or creative life calls her, she cannot be as present to his needs as she formerly was. When sexual differences come to the forefront of the relationship, tensions and misunderstandings often arise. These times of necessary separation enable a man to relate more to his own emotions, and to develop his unrealized potential. If he has the courage to look within and face this period of uncertainty with courage and emotional honesty, instead of blaming his partner for his discomfort, he can enter a deeply rewarding experience. He will also be removing another layer of the Fool's Clothing by embracing his responsibility for developing his own relationship with his inner woman. When he reconnects with his partner, he can relate to her on a new and more mature level. He has learned more about himself during this time of separation, and he now has more of himself to bring to the relationship.

We see in this current encounter with Sigune that Parzival has developed a better relationship with his own soul. Recall that Sigune's demeanor reflects Parzival's relationship to his own soul. Although Sigune still mourns the loss of her beloved, she portrays a sense of peace as she keeps vigil over the tomb of her beloved. During his time of doubt Parzival has learned the importance of developing a relationship with his inner world—he has learned how to renew his Grail Sword. He has accepted deep sorrow as part of his life and he has learned to face and accept his own emotions. Parzival thanks Sigune for her compassion and he begins to follow Cundrie's tracks. However, they soon begin to fade and Parzival is on his own again to find the Grail Castle.

Later that day he meets a Grail Knight who tells Parzival that he is in the land of the Grail Castle. He tries to chase Parzival away and a battle results. Parzival throws the Grail Knight from his horse and the knight runs away to safety. In the contest Parzival's horse slips down a steep embankment and is killed. Fortunately, Parzival grabs a bough and saves himself. He pulls himself back up the embankment and mounts the Grail Knight's horse that remained there, as if it were waiting for Parzival. He is now riding a Grail Knight's horse. Although Parzival still feels lost, he is a different man than the one who left Arthur's court four years before. Instead of becoming a knight of the Round Table, Parzival now rides a Grail horse; he is symbolically moving closer to his destiny at the Grail Castle. Instead of fearing the humiliation of Cundrie's words, Parzival now chooses to follow her trail to the Grail Castle. These events show that Parzival has changed significantly during his period of doubt; they show that he is maturing and is following a path that is more in harmony with his authentic self.

Parzival continues his search for the Grail until one day he encounters another unusual spring snowfall. This snowfall will mark the ending of his period of doubt, just as an earlier snowfall marked its beginning. Parzival is cold as he rides in the snow. Before long he comes upon an old knight and his two daughters walking along the road. The old knight chastises Parzival by telling him that no knight should be wearing armor, because it is a holy day and knights are not allowed to fight on such a day. Parzival tells him that he does not even know what day it is, and that long ago he stopped paying attention to liturgical time—when he stopped serving God. The old knight tells him that it is Good Friday and, since a hermit lives nearby, Parzival ought to go to the hermit and seek counsel. The old knight's daughter now speaks up and implores her father to be kind to Parzival, for she can see that he is freezing in his armor. Her father relents and invites Parzival to stay with them. Though their words and invitation warm Parzival, he would be uncomfortable staying with them since he "hates the One whom they worship." Parzival has not yet resolved his conflict with God—the God in whom his mother taught him to believe.

Parzival politely declines their invitation and rides away from the old knight and his daughters. An immense sorrow overwhelms him. The tale tells us that Parzival not only bears the pain of his failure at the Grail Castle and the pain of his separation from Condwiramurs, but he also bears the sorrow of his father, his mother, and their ancestors. This pain is the final breaking of his ego; it is his personal Good Friday. Parzival lets go of the reins and he thinks, "What if God will give me help to overcome my sadness?" He cries out, "If today be His day of redemption, let Him help me if He can!" For the first time, the son of Herzeloyde with full force feels both his sorrow and the ancestral sorrow he carries within himself. This time Parzival avoids a trance by consciously enduring the pain and sorrow of his life and by reaching beyond himself. As Parzival calls out to God, the Grail horse follows the path that takes him to the cave of a hermit.

The hermit's name is **Trevrizent**. He welcomes Parzival into his cave as his guest and helps him take off his armor. Parzival recognizes this cave, for it was the same cave in which he swore the oath of Jeshute's innocence. Parzival tells the hermit that he had been in this cave years before, and that he took a multicolored spear from the cave that day. Trevrizent says that he knew the knight who owned the spear and that the knight mourned its loss. Parzival asks how long it has been since that day. Trevrizent tells him that it has been four years, six months, and three days. That is how long Parzival has lived in his period of doubt.

Parzival then begins to tell the hermit about his period of doubt. He has lived in despair and has traveled alone. During this time he did not seek a church or a minister. Parzival tells the old man that this time has been a time of battle and strife, and that he bore hatred toward God. The hermit sighs and advises Parzival that bearing hatred toward God is not a very wise idea. Then Trevrizent begins to tell Parzival about himself. He says that he is not a priest but a layman who has experience in the ways of God. He formerly was a knight but in later years he chose a life of religious study. Trevrizent admonishes Parzival to be faithful to God. He says that God is truth, and that one gains nothing by staying angry with Him.

Then Trevrizent begins to teach Parzival about rebellion against God. He tells him that Lucifer's rebellion against God happened at the time of Adam and Eve. He says that the greatest sin for Adam's children, who were driven by discontent, greed, and arrogance, was to rob their grandmother of her virginity. Puzzled by this idea, Parzival asks Trevrizent what he means by "robbing their grandmother of her virginity." Trevrizent replies that the earth was Adam's mother. Adam lived by the fruits of the earth and the earth was a virgin—free from bloodshed. However, when Adam's son Cain killed his brother Abel for a few possessions, blood fell upon the earth for the first time; that is when the earth lost her virginity. From then on hatred sprang up, and it has been the same ever since. Additionally, Trevrizent says that God shares two things with human beings—His love and His hate. Each person can choose between the two and he asks Parzival to consider which would help him more. This is a very interesting view of God, namely, that God turns the same face toward us as we turn toward Him. Psychologically this idea is true. As we have seen in our dream work, energies from the unconscious are hostile toward us if we have rejected them. When these shadow energies first appear in a dream, they seem adversarial to the dreamer. However, if the dreamer accepts these previously rejected shadow energies and consciously relates to them, they appear more friendly in subsequent dreams. If we turn a friendly face toward the unconscious, it responds in kind. If we are negative toward the unconscious, it will present its negative side.

Trevrizent implores Parzival to turn his heart toward God. Parzival tells him that he has tried to serve God, but that all it brought him was sorrow. The hermit asks Parzival to tell him about his sorrow; maybe he can help. Parzival says that his greatest grief is to be separated from the Grail, and then to be separated from his wife. Trevrizent acknowledges that it is a great sorrow to be separated from that which one loves, but that he sees Parzival's separation from Condwiramurs as the greater grief. Then Parzival asks the old man if he has ever seen the Grail. Trevrizent says that he has been in the Grail Castle and has often seen the Grail. Parzival does not have the courage to tell him that he too had been to the Grail Castle, but that he had failed to ask the question that would have healed the King. Parzival does not want another tongue lashing like he received from Cundrie.

Trevrizent then tells Parzival all about the Grail. Every Good Friday a dove comes down from heaven and places a white host in the Grail. Each spring this event renews the power of the Grail for the year. He also tells Parzival the story of how the neutral angels brought the Grail to earth. Parzival then learns about Amfortas and the wound he received when he killed the Pagan Knight. Finally, Trevrizent tells Parzival that one can only come to the Grail if he receives a call. He recalls that once a youth who was not called did come to the Grail Castle. Trevrizent states that this youth was foolish since he did not ask the King the question about his suffering. Parzival is ashamed because Trevrizent is speaking about him.

Trevrizent notices that Parzival rode a Grail Horse to his cave, and he wonders if Parzival has killed a Grail Knight for it. Parzival says that he is the descendant of Gahmuret, and that he would never kill anyone for a Grail horse. However, he does admit that he once killed the Red Knight for his armor. Parzival's words stun Trevrizent. He laments that Parzival has killed his own relative. The Red Knight's wife was the sister of Gahmuret; this means Parzival killed his uncle. Here we see the Cain and Abel motif; Parzival killed another man for a few possessions, thus spilling more blood upon the earth. Trevrizent tells him that through his act of killing the Red Knight, he has committed a serious wrong. He calls Parzival to be conscious of and to acknowledge his guilt.

Parzival is still attempting to absorb the hermit's words when Trevrizent tells him that by his sudden departure, he hastened the death of his own mother. Trevrizent tells Parzival that he knows this because Herzeloyde was his sister. Parzival is shocked to hear Trevrizent's message; he has just discovered that his mother is dead and that Trevrizent is his uncle. Trevrizent then tells Parzival of his heritage. Titurel, Parzival's great-grandfather, was the first Grail King. His son became the next Grail King and he had five children (Two boys: Amfortas and Trevrizent and three girls: Sigune's mother Schoysiane, Parzival's mother Herzeloyde and Repanse de Schoye the Grail Bearer).

Parzival is speechless. After hearing all that Trevrizent has revealed, Parzival confesses to Trevrizent that he was the youth who went to the Grail Castle, and did not ask the question that would have healed the Grail King. Trevrizent is sad and urges Parzival to give up his search for the Grail. He tells Parzival that a person only gets one chance to find the Grail. The old man tells Parzival that as a youth he was a valiant knight who gave up the life of a knight after his brother Amfortas was wounded. He took up the life of a hermit to help atone for his brother's mistake of killing the Pagan Knight. Trevrizent also tells Parzival that he knew Parzival's father Gahmuret very well. In fact, Gahmuret had given him a valuable green stone that now is his altar—the same altar on which Parzival swore his oath four years before. Finally, he tells Parzival that Gahmuret had given him his squire. The squire's name was Ither—the Red Knight whom Parzival has killed. Trevrizent asks Parzival to acknowledge his mistakes: he killed the Red Knight, he hastened his mother's death, and he failed to heal the Grail King when he had the chance. He urges Parzival to do penance and to ask God for forgiveness. This conversation with Trevrizent deeply affects Parzival, and challenges him to take responsibility for his actions.

Parzival stays with Trevrizent for two weeks. During this time of reflection Parzival comes to a deep sense of peace within himself. Just as Gurnemanz was a teacher for Parzival in the ways of knightly life, Trevrizent becomes Parzival's spiritual teacher. At the end of this time Parzival confesses his faults to Trevrizent. Though Trevrizent is not a priest, he says to Parzival, "If you give me your sins, I will take them." Trevrizent absolves Parzival of his mistakes. Freed from his sorrow, Parzival leaves the hermit. However, despite Trevrizent's advice to stop his searching for the Grail, Parzival is more determined than ever to return to the Grail Castle. Parzival is learning to listen to his own inner knowing, and he is developing his own inner authority—the god within.

Parzival's experience with Trevrizent is a powerful one. For us today, a Trevrizent experience is an event that gives us direction, hope, and guidance especially when we are experiencing a period of doubt. Often a Trevrizent experience comes to us through a person, as it did for Parzival. For others it comes through an event, a book, a group experience, or a retreat. No matter how it comes, the Trevrizent experience helps us gain insight into ourselves and helps us resolve the dilemmas of our life during a particularly difficult time. The Trevrizent experience helps us to discover a new way of being and a new perspective on our life. An essential ingredient of this experience is that the seeker must be psychologically honest, that is, he must accept his past actions without rationalizations or excuses. To look honestly at our life with its successes and its failures takes courage, but it also brings us freedom. Those in twelve-step programs know this experience. The fifth step is sharing a fearless, moral inventory with a trusted person. A Trevrizent experience can be a time of personal insight that gives us a clearer view of our identity. One looks back over one's life and sees the successes and the failures, only this time not from the point of view of the ego, but from the point of view of the Self. Acknowledgment of the truth, acceptance of responsibility for one's actions, and a genuine remorse bring self-forgiveness, freedom, and a renewed spirit. Often, like Parzival, we can gain a new spiritual point of view as we emerge from our period of doubt.

Parzival's Trevrizent experience takes place on Good Friday. In the Christian liturgical life, Good Friday is the time of death that precedes the new life that Easter brings. In the esoteric understanding of the Christian myth, the emphasis is not so much on Christ as the one who atones for sin, but on Christ as the model for the way to live an authentic life. Living our unique, personal destiny is not an easy task. Jung once said:

> Are we to understand the "imitation of Christ" in the sense that we should copy his life and, if I may use the expression, ape his stigmata; or in the deeper sense that we are to live our own proper lives as truly as he lived his in its individual uniqueness? It is no easy matter to live a life that is modeled

on Christ's, but it is unspeakably harder to live our own life as truly as Christ lived his.[3]

In the natural world spring always follows winter. The laws of nature and human nature are the same. Therefore, the mystery of death and new life naturally seeks to occur within our psyche. This great mystery of death to the old ways and opening to the previously unknown life must take place repeatedly in every human soul, if it is to evolve. Psychologically, death is the giving up of the way the ego wants to live. Often we discover that we have developed a false identity to cope with or adjust to our family and our society. This false self is not who we are as a soul. The new life is formed when we begin to take seriously the deep soul identity that wants to be manifested though us. When we open ourselves to our soul identity, we begin living from the point of view of the Self. This attitude of surrendering and reaching out to the Self is what ultimately releases us from the period of doubt, as Parzival displays. An attitude of surrender consists of a lifelong series of dying to our ego consciousness and opening and surrendering to that which is bigger than we are. We often need help to make this transformation. The help comes from wise and loving people around us and from the wisdom of our inner world, the world of dreams.

The Questions

1. Think about a time in your life when you experienced a period of doubt. Write about this time. What was it like for you? How did you deal with it? What did you learn from it?

2. Remember a time when you were separated from your partner—either physically or emotionally. Could you see this as an opportunity to relate to your inner world and your own inner feminine? If so, what did you learn about yourself?

3. Who or what events have been a Trevrizent experience for you? Who or what events have helped you get a new insight into yourself and helped you discover your true nature during a period of doubt? Write about this experience.

4. Have you made peace with your past?

5. Do you see the mystery of death and new life as a force running through your life? If so, write about your experience.

6. How do you experience God? How have your images of God changed over the years? Write about this.

Chapter Eight

Gawain: Self-knowledge Through Relationship
Inner Life

As we have seen in the dreams we have examined so far, dreams show us a situation and our current response to it, but they do not always have a resolution. Even if we can see the pattern or the meaning of the dream, we are often left with many unanswered questions. Jung devised a method to deal with this situation. He taught that we can return to a dream while we are awake, and interact with it and its characters to discover a deeper meaning or to address unanswered questions. Jung called this method active imagination. Whereas in a dream we are unconsciously experiencing the dream action, in active imagination we are awake, making conscious choices, and interacting with the images from the dream. The interaction takes place on the imaginative level. We call this process active imagination because the ego is actively involved—we go back into the inner world and interact with the images and characters there. We are actively questioning, arguing with, being supported by, and making peace with the people and images we find there. By doing so, we are consciously interacting with a previously unknown part of ourselves.

Let us return for a moment to the dreams presented in previous chapters. In my dream about pushing the man in the wheelchair into the off-limits area, I could go back and talk to the man in the bed who just woke up, and find out more about him. David could go back, learn more about Castor Troy, and discover how this shadow energy is working in his life. Peter could go back and examine the nature of the evil spirit and why it is troubling him so. When we do active imagination things change in the psyche. The relationship between our conscious self and the unconscious is altered—the interaction changes both. We change because we are relating to and accepting previously unknown parts of ourselves. Images from the unconscious transform into their more positive side when we accept them. For a thorough and rich discussion of active imagination, I suggest reading Robert Johnson's book *Inner Work*. I will summarize some important elements of this method.

Active imagination is often done in writing. It is important that we use some form or method that brings the interaction from the mental world into the physical world. By doing so we ground the experience in the outer world, and make it more likely that we can assimilate the experience into our waking life. Some people find it easier to have the active imagination experience through mental imagery and then write it down immediately. Others embody the active imagination experience through dance, making music or sculpture, or speaking it aloud. Each person will discover the method that works for him to deepen and expand his dream experience. Where you do active imagination is important. Find a place where you can be alone and undisturbed, so you will have the freedom to express yourself without feeling self-conscious or having the need to edit your experience. Some people light a candle as a way of ritually beginning the experience of active imagination and extinguish the candle to mark its end.

Robert Johnson gives four steps in the process of active imagination. I will review them and then give you an example. The first step is the invitation. When you find a private setting, clear your mind and invite an image from a recent dream back into your consciousness. Wait attentively and relinquish control about how the interaction will go. Be open to learning something new.

The second step is the dialogue. With the attitude of being willing to listen, begin by addressing questions to the dream character. Open-ended questions are the best. Some possible questions are: What have you come to tell me? What do you need from me? Can you tell me something about yourself? Is there something you want to tell me about how you see me? What part of me are you? Where are you operating in my life? Why are you doing such and such in my dream? Where in my body do I feel the energy of this image? Participate in the dialogue with your feelings. If the figure says something that touches you or angers you, express that emotion to the character and wait for its reaction. Allow the character to have its own personality different from yours. Johnson suggests that we learn to listen and not to approach the process with a prepared script. If the interaction surprises you, you are probably doing it correctly. Sometimes the character does not speak, but expresses itself in action. If it does, respond to it with your own feelings or actions. In the inner world animals and objects can speak and react to us. Write down whatever takes place in the dialogue or action.

The third step is bringing your values to the dialogue. Jung taught that humanity has an important role to play in creation—to bring human values to life. The forces of nature with all their power and beauty are nonetheless amoral. They do not bring forth our sense of human justice, fairness, and care for one another. It is our job as human beings to bring these values to the active imagination. Johnson cites an example from Jung's practice. A man told Jung a dream in which he saw his girlfriend drowning in icy waters. Jung advised the man to return to the dream through active imagination, rescue the drowning and ignored feminine part of himself from the icy waters, and build a fire to help her dry off and regain warmth. By doing so the dreamer might find a way to become more related to his inner feminine. Jung also suggests that it is just as important to rescue the figures in our unconscious as it is for us to rescue people in the outer world. Johnson encourages the person who attempts active imagination to hold out for the attitude and conduct that are consistent with his character and deepest values. When conflicting points of view occur in a dream, he encourages us to take a stance that holds both sides of the conflict without denying either side of us. It is our job as a dreamer to bring these values into play as we interact with the dream characters.

The fourth step is ritual—the same as the fourth step of Johnson's dream work method. The purpose of this step is to perform an action that brings the experience of the active imagination into the physical world. Ritual helps to ground the experience and makes it more possible to integrate the meaning of the active imagination work into our concrete life. We can develop a ritual to honor the message of a dream and may later design a new ritual to honor the additional meaning gained through active imagination.

More than twenty years ago I dreamed that I was walking near a lake and I was carrying a fishing pole that I had received from my sister. When I put the line into the water, a very large fish came to the surface. The size of the fish frightened me and I awoke. Obviously this dream was unfinished and contained significant energy that frightened me. It knew that I ought to find out what this fish wanted from me, and why I was so frightened of it. I took my journal to a quiet place, and invited the image of the fish to be with me. I asked it who it was and it responded that it was an angelfish. "What do you want from me?" I asked. "I want you to come with me." was the reply. In my imagination I entered the water and held onto the angelfish. It plunged deep into the water as I held onto its back. Down to the bottom of the lake we went. Fortunately in active imagination one can breathe under water. The fish took me to an underground cave. A woman wearing a veil came out of the cave. I began a conversation with her. She told me some things about myself that I had not realized. She challenged me about how I was relating to some people in my life—keeping them at a distance with an intellectual approach. In some ways her challenge was a mild form of a Cundrie experience. I listened to her and took her challenge seriously. I recorded our conversation in my journal. Often in the next months I went to a body of water in my neighborhood, and walked around it as a ritual to honor that active imagination. There I would think about the message I had received from the woman at the bottom of the lake and sometimes I would continue the conversation with her. Over time my friendships with others became warmer and more genuine. I had the woman to thank for this change in me and, of course, my angelfish who led me to her. After doing the active imagination I recalled that the location of the lake in the dream was a prep school in another state. The school was called "Our Lady of the Lake." My dream had a sense of humor and a profound reality for me to explore.

Johnson gives two important cautionary notes about active imagination. He says it is wise, if you are going to do active imagination on your own, to have an experienced person or therapist to help you in case you get stuck. Most people can do active imagination on their own, but because the unconscious is so powerful, sometimes a person may have a hard time turning off the images and returning to his everyday life. In such a case having an experienced person to turn to for guidance is important. Johnson's second caution refers to the fact that our dream will often use the image of a person we know in the outer life to show us one of our unconscious qualities. In other words we may dream of our wife, or friend, or colleague who represents one of our unaccepted qualities. Do not dialogue with that image. It is too easy to get the dream image mixed up with the person we know in the outer life. Johnson advises that we ask the image to change slightly, so we can distinguish it as part of our own psyche, and separate the dream image from the human being in our outer life. When the image changes, then we can dialogue with it knowing that we are relating to some part of our own psyche and not that other human being. Sometimes the image might change clothes, hairstyle, its name, or form to help us distinguish it from the outer life.

Experiment with this method and see if your dreams will have more meaning and richness for you. For a man to spend time and energy learning to relate to his own psyche is a very noble and worthy task that will improve his relationship with himself. Additionally, it will improve his relationship with those he loves and with the larger community to which he belongs. Doing active imagination is a concrete way for a man to develop his skill with his second sword—the sword of the inner life.

The Story and Commentary

The adventures of Gawain within the Parzival tale seem like a completely separate story. The Gawain section has its own cast of characters and its own unique plot. However, Gawain's adventures are an integral part of the Parzival tale. Ever since the day on the snowy meadow when Gawain helped Parzival out of the trance, and rode with him into Arthur's court, these two men remained linked as brothers. During the more than four years that Parzival endures his period of doubt, Gawain takes the center stage of the story. Parzival weaves in and out of Gawain's tales, but for the most part, Parzival's presence in the tale is peripheral. During a period of doubt most of a person's energy is unavailable for outer life activities. The psyche is undergoing a major reorganization, so that much of the psyche's energy is active within—below the level of consciousness. During these times a person often experiences malaise. Wolfram portrays Parzival's period of doubt by keeping him in the background of the story while Gawain and his adventures take a center stage. As previously stated, Gawain and Parzival represent two distinct parts of human nature. Parzival's way is the path of self-knowledge through the inner way. Gawain's is the path of self-knowledge through love and relationship—the outer way. To reach the Grail we need both.

Though Parzival is in the background during this part of the tale, Wolfram uses several incidents to emphasize the link between Gawain and Parzival. At one point Parzival and Gawain find themselves on opposite sides of a battle. Fortunately, Gawain recognizes Parzival in time and no harm is done. Gawain loses his horse in another battle. Later, Parzival comes to that town with his wounded horse. He trades his horse for a healthy horse that happens to be Gawain's lost horse. Parzival rides Gawain's horse.

Recall that on the day Cundrie came to Arthur's camp and confronted Parzival, a knight also arrived and challenged Gawain to defend his name. The knight accused Gawain of killing a lord. Gawain reaches a complicated truce with this knight instead of doing battle with him. While discussing the terms of the truce, Gawain hears a remarkable tale. A noble knight had earlier defeated Gawain's adversary; the noble knight was Parzival. Gawain's opponent, in exchange for his life, promised Parzival to seek the Grail for one year. If the knight were unsuccessful, he would go to a certain kingdom and present himself to Queen Condwiramurs. The knight was to tell Condwiramurs that her husband sent him to be at her service, and that Parzival has much sorrow because of their separation. Thus, Gawain discovers that Parzival had defeated his opponent. As part of the truce with his adversary Gawain agrees to take on that knight's responsibility, in other words, Gawain agrees to search for the Grail. By this complicated turn of events we see that Gawain has now undertaken Parzival's task—searching for the Grail. Meanwhile Parzival is riding Gawain's horse. The fates of Gawain and Parzival are deeply intertwined.

As Gawain continues his adventure, he often recalls Parzival's parting words to him on the day they left Arthur's camp. Parzival wished that the inspiration and protection that come from a good wife would be a guide for his friend Gawain. One day Gawain approaches a castle built high up on a mountaintop. This is the Castle of Wonders, the one to which Cundrie had referred. In this castle someone has imprisoned four queens and four hundred maidens. However, before getting to the castle, Gawain meets a beautiful woman named **Orgeluse.** Her beauty is so striking that only Condwiramurs' can compare. Gawain is smitten and offers Orgeluse his love. She rejects his offer. Gawain takes an interesting tactic; he refuses to accept the rejection. He tells Orgeluse that by rejecting him she is damaging her own property, since he already belongs to her. Gawain will not allow himself to be rejected—so sure is he of his love for her. Orgeluse then sets out many tasks for Gawain to test his love. In fact she is quite antagonistic and demeaning of him. However, Gawain is unfazed. He tells her that she may have a bad temper now, but that he is certain that her graciousness will follow. It is very tempting, while reading this section of the story, to see Orgeluse as an abusive woman and Gawain as a co-dependent male. However, Wolfram warns his readers not to judge Orgeluse too harshly until we know her true heart.

Gawain and Orgeluse approach the Castle of Wonders, a symbol of the repressed feminine. The feminine, as we have been speaking of it, refers not to females but to the feminine qualities within the psyche of men and women. Some of these qualities include the feeling function, valuing relating, intuition, valuing the body and its inner wisdom, and seeking the essence of love instead of power over others. These feminine qualities are the ones that the patriarchy has repressed. This repression has resulted in the injuring of the feminine spirit in both men and women. As a symbol of this repression, the castle has the four queens and four hundred maidens trapped inside. The King of the

Castle of Wonders is **Clinschor**, who is the symbol of the patriarchy. Many years before Clinschor was caught in an illicit affair with another man's wife. In retaliation the husband castrated Clinschor who has been embittered ever since. He uses all his powers against men and women, and especially against love. Again in our story we see Wolfram emphasizing the opposites. The Castle of Wonders stands in contrast to the Grail Castle. Both Kings are wounded in the same manner—castration. However, their response to the wound is completely different. Amfortas suffers his wound, while Clinschor makes others suffer. It becomes Gawain's task to free the Castle of Wonders and its feminine energy.

A boatman ferries Orgeluse across a river to the Castle of Wonders. She remains ill-tempered, and will not allow Gawain to join her in the boat. Gawain has to wait, and then he has to defeat a knight to earn his passage across the river. He does so. Since it is the end of the day, the boatman invites Gawain to stay at his home for the night. In the morning he will ferry Gawain across the river. Gawain gratefully accepts the boatman's offer. The next morning as Gawain looks out upon the castle, he wonders how the maidens became trapped there. He asks the boatman's daughter if she knows. She is horrified that he has asked this question, and so is her father. Unlike the situation at the Grail Castle, at the Castle of Wonders one was not to ask questions. Still Gawain persists. Eventually the boatman yields and tells Gawain what a horrible place the castle is, and tells him that severe trials await anyone who enters the castle. He tells Gawain about the bed in the castle called the Bed of Wonders. If anyone can endure the trials on the Bed of Wonders, he will be the Lord of the Castle and the women will be freed. The boatman gives Gawain his shield, and tells him always to hold this shield and his sword if he encounters the Bed of Wonders.

After the boatman ferries Gawain across the river, he approaches the Castle of Wonders. He enters the beautifully adorned castle, but he sees no maidens. Gawain enters a large room with a floor that is as slippery as glass. In the center of the room is the Bed of Wonders on rollers. It is moving around the room. Gawain is not sure how to mount this moving bed, but he knows it is his task. So with shield and sword in hand he leaps upon the bed. Suddenly a deafening roar fills the hall and the bed moves violently, crashing into all four walls. Gawain hangs on and prays to God for help. Suddenly the bed stops in the center of the room and all is quiet—but not for long. Huge stones are hurled at Gawain from all directions. He does his best to block them with his shield, but some of them hit him. Following the stones five hundred arrows fly directly at him. Gawain hides under his shield, pierced by many arrows. He survives these onslaughts, but he is cut and bruised. A giant then enters the room carrying a club. He tells Gawain not to fear him because danger will not come from him. As the giant leaves, a huge lion as tall as a horse rushes in. By this time Gawain is on his feet and defends himself with his shield against the lion's first blow. The lion's claw pierces the shield. Gawain uses his sword to cut off one of the lion's legs. Yet the fight is far from over. The lion continues his attack so fiercely that Gawain can feel its breath on his face. Finally, Gawain uses his sword to wound the lion fatally. Blood covers the hall. The battle exhausts Gawain and he collapses onto the slain lion.

How are we to understand the Bed of Wonders and the battle Gawain fights? When one encounters the Bed of Wonders one is encountering his own unconscious; for our bed is the place where we nightly meet our unconscious. This encounter is very disorienting and difficult. The moving and shaking bed represent this disorientation. The hurled rocks are the thoughts we find in our unconscious. The arrows are the many emotions that come toward us, when we are assailed by the unconscious. The lion is our huge, instinctive animal nature that we must face and learn to integrate into our lives. The animal nature is the side of us that operates purely out of our instincts, such as hunger, sex, creativity, the drive for meaning, and aggression. Our animal nature wants what it wants and it wants it now. These animal instincts are necessary parts of us. However, these powerful forces can easily overwhelm us, and then we act as a crude animal and a thug in the world. If we can face these forces within ourselves and not be overwhelmed by them, some of our repressed feminine qualities are freed and we can use them creatively in our life. Working with our dreams is our way of riding the Bed of Wonders. There we are confronted with our many, unruly thoughts, our numerous emotions, and our instinctive animal nature. It takes a brave and skilled man to endure this experience. We need the skill of using our second sword to win this battle with our unconscious.

Gawain does a very good job thanks to his courage, strength, and the boatman's shield. However, his work is not yet complete. In alchemy the seeker ultimately learns to ride the lion, not to kill it.[1] Nevertheless, Gawain accomplishes a great feat during his first encounter with the Bed of Wonders—he survives. Eventually he will need to learn how to make peace with his instinctive, animal nature. This is an important and difficult task for any man. In fact, we cannot open to the fullness of our spiritual potential unless we accept and integrate our instinctive animal nature. For example, we cannot be a true pacifist if we do not first experience that within us is also a murderous and violent side. We must know in our bones that we could and would kill and harm others with our aggression before we can adopt a pacifist stance in the world. Without this integration of our aggressive nature, pacifism would be an ideal that we could speak about, but that would fail us when put to the test. Remember that on the day of his wounding, Amfortas left the castle under the banner of Love. However, when he met the pagan knight, his murderous side prevailed. Since his aggressive side had not been integrated, the ideal of love was of no practical value to him. Without this integration, love is merely an idea and not its authentic, embodied essence.

When Gawain collapses in exhaustion, the four queens of the castle approach, bandage him, and nurse him back to health. Gawain sleeps the whole day and through the night. The next morning he awakens to the four queens who are still caring for him. Gawain discovers that the oldest queen is Arthur's mother, another is her daughter, and the final two are his lost sisters. Gawain and his kin enjoy a warm and joyful reunion. The feminine locked in the castle is not only Gawain's personal feminine, but also that of previous generations—the collective feminine. The Castle of Wonders is a symbol today for the systematic and widespread repression of healthy feminine values in our Western culture. We, like Gawain, have the task of facing the struggles within our unconscious, and freeing our imprisoned feminine energy.

In the castle Gawain also discovers a magic pillar that reveals what is taking place within six miles of the Castle. Gawain looks into it and sees Orgeluse with another knight. Jealousy and anger overwhelm him. He has not yet learned to ride the lion, that is, his passions overwhelm him. Gawain rushes out, crosses the river, and defeats the knight. Orgeluse is still reluctant to accept Gawain's love, and she gives him another task. This time Gawain must cross a huge ravine. On the other side is a certain tree from which he must take a bough, make a wreath, and bring it back to Orgeluse.

Gawain willingly accepts the task. He mounts his horse, leaps across the ravine, and falls into a swift river. Fortunately, both Gawain and his horse are good swimmers. When they get to the other side, Gawain finds the tree and takes the branch that he makes into a wreath. Gawain is ready to return to Orgeluse when a huge man confronts him. The man is named **Gramoflanz**; he is the guardian of the special tree. Gramoflanz always seeks combat with whoever removes a branch from the tree. Gramoflanz is an exceptional warrior who rarely fights one man at a time; he prefers to battle up to five men at once. Before challenging

Gawain, Gramoflanz tells him that he knows about the task that Gawain is doing for Orgeluse. This task was once his task. Gramoflanz once loved Orgeluse and killed her first husband in battle. He stopped loving her, and now he loves a queen from the Castle of Wonders. He asks Gawain to be his messenger and to deliver a ring to the queen for whom he now pines. Gawain does not tell Gramoflanz that the queen he desires is his own sister. In their conversation Gramoflanz learns of Gawain's lineage. Gawain's father had killed Gramoflanz's father in a battle years before. When Gramoflanz discovers who Gawain's father is, he becomes furious and vows to avenge his father's death. He challenges Gawain to meet him in a battle in sixteen days at an agreed-upon site. Gawain accepts the challenge.

With the bough in his hand Gawain mounts his horse and leaps across the ravine—this time without falling in. Gawain gives the wreath to Orgeluse. When she receives the wreath, her demeanor changes. She opens to his love and declares her love for Gawain. She weeps when she recalls her deceased husband whom Gramoflanz killed. Then, as often happens when one opens the heart to another, Orgeluse confesses her secrets. She was the woman who had an illicit affair with Amfortas before his fateful wounding. She also tells Gawain that she met Parzival and tried to seduce him. However, unlike Amfortas, Parzival refused her advances. This detail of the story tells the reader that Parzival has faced some of the same challenges as Amfortas, and that he is surpassing the wounded Grail King. Parzival has learned to tame and refine his lust, his animal instinct.

Gawain and Orgeluse now ride back to the Castle of Wonders, and they take their place as its King and Queen. Gawain sends a message back to Arthur's court inviting him and his company to be present for his battle with Gramoflanz. He intends to surprise Arthur by reuniting him with his mother. Within several days Arthur and his court arrive at the castle. The reunion between Arthur and his mother is a beautiful one. They hold a great feast. The conversations and the love expressed between Arthur's men and the four hundred ladies of the castle are rich and meaningful for all. Never before have men and women shared such warmth. Orgeluse's love brings a deep healing and satisfaction to Gawain. Her antagonism is gone as her true nature is revealed. The ways of Clinschor are reversed. Men and woman are uniting and are in harmony with one another instead of being at odds. The patriarchy has lost its deadly hold on the castle. The masculine and the feminine are enriching each other as it is meant to be.

As previously stated Gawain's path is self-knowledge through love and commitment. Gawain needs courage, commitment, and tremendous consciousness to pass the tests of love and relationship. We need the same qualities if we are to pass the test of love. Modern psychology helps us understand the unconscious dynamics that occur in love relationships. Child psychology is teaching us how extremely tender-hearted and impressionable a child is. Over time children have to repress many of their emotional response and wounds because of lack of awareness or insensitivity of their parents. When children feel emotionally unsafe, they learn to repress their natural responses to function within a family system. What we repressed in our childhood, and continue to repress today becomes our personal four hundred maidens trapped in the Castle of Wonders. Much of our life force and creative energy becomes blocked in this process of repression. As children we personalize and internalize our experiences, and we adopt some false conclusions about ourselves. When our environment is unable to respond adequately to our emotion needs, we can easily come to believe that we do not deserve love or that there is something wrong with us. Many children draw unfortunate conclusions about intimacy: if I get close, the other person will not respond to my needs, or if I get close, the other person will impose their will upon me. These unconscious beliefs make intimate relationships very difficult and open to much misunderstanding and defensiveness. When we enter a committed relationship our unconscious beliefs, fears, and childhood deprivation are activated—we find ourselves challenged to endure our own Bed of Wonders.

As we have seen, the Self wants us free. It wants our repressed emotions and creativity free, and it wants our repressed feminine life force available to us. The deeper purpose of a committed relationship is to heal the hurts and wounds that were created in our childhood. The mystery of attraction, in part, is life's way of helping us free our repressed energy. Therefore, we find ourselves attracted to people who, because of their personality and because of their wounds, will help us experience the pain and discomfort that we could not allow ourselves to experience as children. In this way life gives us another chance to learn about ourselves, to heal our wounds, and to mature. However, since our unfortunate beliefs about intimacy are unconscious, our partner will often seem like an enemy instead of the person life has given us to evoke our repressed material. Orgeluse first experienced Gawain that way; his love for her evoked the pain of her previous losses in love, and she protected herself from this pain by her antagonistic attitude.

Relationship is quite difficult if we see our partner as the cause of our pain and discomfort instead of the person whose love is bringing our pain to consciousness. Moreover, what makes love relationships even more trying is that the dynamic of blaming the partner for one's own unconscious pain happens both ways. I am also evoking my partner's repressed material and appearing as the enemy. It takes a tremendous amount of consciousness and commitment for a person to endure these trials. What we are experiencing in these times of conflict with our partner is our own unconscious material. Like Gawain our task is to experience our own Bed of Wonders — to deal with our own unconscious. At these times of conflict with our partner, our own repressed thoughts, emotions, and instinctive animal nature can overwhelm us.

The following story is an example of a man Sam, whose repressed childhood pain reemerged in his committed relationship. Sam's girlfriend had a cat. From the first day he met her cat, Sam was hostile toward it and the male cat was equally antagonistic toward him. Even after he married his girlfiend and took her cat into his home, the stand-off continued. Years later in his therapy, Sam remembered that, as a boy, he had a cat whom he loved. One day his cat became ill; the next day the cat was gone and Sam never saw it again. No one in Sam's home ever spoke to him about his cat and its fate. Several days later, Sam heard his mother talking to a neighbor as she described how she took his dying cat to the veterinarian to mercifully put it to death. In an ill-advised attempt to protect her son, Sam's mother failed to help him feel and process the grief and pain that occur when a boy opens his heart to love and then experiences a loss. As a result Sam unconsciously closed his heart to cats — the symbol of his unresolved grief and pain. As we can imagine, Sam's close-heartedness to his wife's dear cat caused her confusion and sadness; it created a tension between them. Sam's conflict with the cat and with his wife surfaced because of his own unresolved pain and grief. These emotions are represented by the arrows on the Bed of Wonders. Because of Sam's consciousness and courage to face his own pain, he found healing. Years later when his wife's cat became fatally ill, Sam went to the veterinarian's office with her. He supported and comforted his wife as she said goodbye to her beloved pet; Sam gave her the presence and care that his mother did not give him. Sam even spent the extra money to have her cat cremated, so that they could bring the ashes back to their home for his wife and their daughters to bury in the backyard. Recently, Sam, his wife, and their daughters welcomed a new cat into their home. He reports how he enjoys and loves the new cat. His change of heart is pleasing to his wife — the cat conflict has vanished. When a man consciously endures the trials on his Bed of Wonders, healing occurs. His feminine warmth and values have returned. Sam has reclaimed his original self—the open and loving self he was as a boy.

Learning to face our own repressed material is a great accomplishment for any of us. The lost feminine life force within us is not freed without this work. In addition, it is a tremendous blessing to have a partner who is willing to bring consciousness to the relationship by facing his or her own repressed pain, and helping us face ours. If a couple can do this work together, not only are they freeing and improving their own lives, but also they are affecting and changing the whole collective situation. They have done their part in clearing the world of a little more darkness and bringing more consciousness and love to our planet. If you cannot remember your dreams, you can still work with your unconscious and come to know yourself. Facing your own thoughts, emotions, and animal instinct as they surface when you are in a conflict with your partner is an effective way of engaging in this process. Every week I have the privilege of working with couples who are attempting to bring consciousness and caring to their relationships. When in conflict, if the couple can learn to create an emotional space in which both of their subjective emotional experiences can be stated, held as equally valuable, validated, and cared about, then each of them will experience a deep sense of connection to their authentic feeling self and to each other. By creating this emotional safety for one another, they are helping the other heal his or her childhood hurts. They are helping each other to face their own Bed of Wonders and to free their repressed feminine energy. This work requires great love, courage, and commitment. Besides themselves, their children and loved ones are the beneficiaries of this work.

Additionally, when two people engage in this healing process, they are making it possible for each other to engage in an even deeper work. Once our previously repressed emotions are validated and allowed to consciously live, the next step in soul development requires us to remove our projections of God from our partner and from other social and religious people. By doing so, we will be claiming our own inner authority. Often we need another to first see and validate us until we can learn to validate ourselves and live from our own inner truth and knowing. After we have endured Gawain's task in our life, we can then focus on Parzival's task—to experience and claim the god within.

Let us return to Gawain's next challenge. It is the appointed day for the battle with Gramoflanz. Gawain goes out early to the place of battle, where he sees a man riding with a wreath on his head. He thinks it is Gramoflanz, but it is Parzival who has also obtained a branch from the tree Gramoflanz guarded. Gawain attacks Parzival and a fierce battle ensues. At the point when Parzival is defeating Gawain, a squire happens by and calls out Gawain's name. Parzival realizes whom he is fighting and stops. He feels sorrow and remorse for harming his dear friend. He is attending to Gawain's wounds when Gramoflanz appears for the battle. Parzival's blows have so weakened Gawain that he cannot fight Gramoflanz. Parzival offers to fight Gramoflanz in his place. Gawain insists that it be his battle and that he will face Gramoflanz the next day when he has recovered. Gramoflanz agrees to delay the battle one day.

Gawain invites Parzival back to Arthur's camp with him. Parzival is very timid about returning to Arthur's court, because four years before he was humiliated by Cundrie in front of the court. Despite his apprehension, Parzival is persuaded to join Gawain. Much to Parzival's surprise, the entire court welcomes him warmly. They have not lost their respect for his courage and valor. In fact, by the end of the day, all the Knights of the Round Table agree to help Parzival search for the Grail. This is an important moment in our tale. Instead of Parzival's becoming a knight of the Round Table, the Knights now are Grail Searchers. Parzival has found his true path, and the Knights of the Round Table whose company Parzival once wanted to join, now support him on his unique journey. When a person is living from the place of the Self, opportunities come his way, doors open effortlessly, and support is available to him.

Parzival finds comfort and joy in his reunion with Arthur's court, but he remains troubled that he has injured Gawain, and he fears that his friend will be too weak for the next battle. Parzival begs Arthur to allow him instead of Gawain to fight Gramoflanz. However, Arthur sides with Gawain and denies Parzival's request. Early the next morning Gramoflanz is waiting in the field. Parzival still feels responsible for Gawain's weakened condition. Therefore, he defies Arthur's wishes and sneaks out of camp to fight Gramoflanz. It is a ferocious battle. Gramoflanz who has rarely fought less than two men before, now feels as if he is fighting against six. Parzival is about to defeat Gramoflanz when Arthur and Gawain arrive and stop the battle. Gramoflanz vows that he will never again face two or more combatants—he has met his match. Since Gramoflanz is in no condition for another battle this day, all the men return to Arthur's camp.

Meanwhile, Gawain's sister has quite an internal conflict. She has accepted the ring from Gramoflanz and has returned his love. She loves her brother Gawain too, and she does not want to see either man hurt or killed in battle. Through a series of negotiations facilitated by several women, including Queen Ginover, the men yield to the feeling function of Gawain's sister and call a truce. Gawain and Gramoflanz embrace and exchange a kiss to mark the truce. "Hatred melted like snow in the sun." This moment shows the power of the feminine—the feeling function rules the day. The value of life is confirmed. Alternatives to battles can be found when the repressed feminine is freed.

With this matter settled, Arthur's court prepares for a great wedding feast. Four couples are to be wed: Gawain and Orgeluse, Gawain's sister and Gramoflanz, and two other couples. Tremendous joy and peace fill the men of Arthur's court and the women from the Castle of Wonders. They have overcome the cruel and unfeeling ways of Clinschor and the patriarchy.

The next day, as the wedding feast is about to begin, Parzival feels how much he misses his wife Condwiramurs. He sees the joy of this day and longs to share it with her. The pain seems too much for Parzival to bear, so he mounts his horse and rides away from the feast to face his final adventure.

The Questions

1. Think about Gawain's experience of the bed in the Castle of Wonders as a metaphor for wrestling with the forces of the unconscious. In your committed relationship have you ever had such an encounter with your inner forces (unconscious)? If so, what thoughts and emotions were activated? How did you deal with them? Write about this.

2. What is your relationship with your instinctive animal nature (the lion)? Does it defeat you? Do you kill it off? Have you learned to ride on its back? Write about this.

3. Look at yourself when you are in a committed relationship. Can you see you wound that is attempting to be healed? Can you see your partners? What are you learning about yourself in this relationship?

4. Feeling function: the side of the personality that makes choices based primarily on what one values from the heart— not necessarily logical. What do you really value in your life? What actions show you that this is true?

5. Take a dream character and do active imagination with it. Follow Robert Johnson's method: invitation, dialogue, value, and ritual.

Chapter Nine

Making Peace With Your Brother and Coming Home

Inner Life

If you have gotten this far in the book and are still saying to yourself, "I do not remember my dreams," or "I will not be able to do this work," you are not alone. Several men who have taken this course have been in the same position. Other men after six or seven weeks will proudly report that they could remember their first dream. Some people simply have a difficult time remembering their dreams despite their best efforts. However, there are other ways of developing an inner life, if dreams are not available. If you have been journaling and answering the questions at the end of each chapter, you are working on your relationship with your inner life.

Another excellent way for us to develop our inner life is to work with our projections. A projection is the unconscious process of seeing something of ourselves in another person. We know we are engaged in a projection when we have an intense emotional reaction to certain qualities in another person.

For example, I may have a neighbor who is quite self-centered. Maybe he rakes his leaves so that they blow into my yard, and he borrows my tools but does not remember to return them. He may ask me to help him on a project, but is not available when I need his help. No one would like to be treated this way and one would easily become angry about this kind of behavior. However, if my reaction to my neighbor is excessive—if I complain about him whenever I have a chance, if I find myself thinking about him often and imagine that I am telling him off, or if I have some sleepless nights ruminating about him—then I am experiencing a projection. I am seeing in my neighbor one of my qualities that I have not accepted, or whose existence I have denied. My self-centered neighbor is giving me an opportunity to work on myself, and to get to know myself better. When I recognize this projection, I can have a dialogue (active imagination) with the self-centered part of myself. Remember I do not dialogue with the image of my neighbor, but with my self-centered side. I might not act in the same manner that my neighbor does, nevertheless, through this dialogue I might discover that my self-centered side is expressed in my relationship with my wife. I might see that I want her to do things my way, to think like I think, and to respond to life as I do. What an awakening that would be to discover that I have qualities that are similar to those of my neighbor whom I cannot stand. If I then have the courage to admit this fact to myself, and to accept that I have a part of me that really is self-centered, then I can correct myself and not let this self-centered part of me cause havoc in my marriage. Remember that there is nothing wrong with me when I discover that I have a self-centered side—it is simply part of being a human being. I am like the magpie: some black feathers along with some white feathers. It becomes a problem when I pretend that I do not have a self-centered side, because then I will unknowingly be self-centered with my wife and self-righteously condemn my neighbor for being so defective. Projections that remain unconscious or not withdrawn are a major cause of the problems on our planet. What I cannot accept in myself, I will condemn in another—with rigor and righteousness. However, if I can embrace and learn to deal with my projections, I will have more compassion and understanding for others and their weaknesses. The world will be a more peaceful place, when more people work with and accept their projections. Therefore, if you do not remember your dreams, work on your projections. If you do remember your dreams, work on your projections.

We project not only our black feathers onto others, but we also project our white feathers. When I see someone whom I admire, and I have an excessive reaction to him or her, it is a good sign that I am seeing some of my own unaccepted qualities in that person. For example, I may admire a person for his creativity. Most people are moved and impressed when seeing the work of a creative person. However, if my reaction is excessive—I talk about his work to whoever will listen, I attend every presentation this person gives, and I fantasize about being with him and becoming his best friend—then I know that I am also seeing some of my unaccepted creativity in him. The correct response to this realization is to begin a dialogue with my creative side. In the dialogue I might ask my creative side to describe itself to me, where it wants to express itself through me, and what beliefs about myself I might have to give up to accept it. I may discover that my creativity is in a completely different area than that of the person I so admire. Nonetheless, it is creative energy that wants to be expressed through me. If a man works regularly on owning his projections and accepting the psychic energy that is really his, instead of projecting it onto other people, his life will become richer and more fulfilling.

I want to give you another example of active imagination. Joe, a 52-year-old therapist, had the following dream:

> I am in a castle with two women. We are separated for a time and then reunited. Later I make a big salad. I announce that I have gone to a cooking class and we are learning to make salads. I prepare a beautiful salad in a very large bowl. The younger woman takes a small pitcher of salad dressing and begins to pour it onto the salad in the bowl. When she has poured about 1/3 of the dressing, I tell her to stop. Nevertheless, she continues to pour. I tell her to stop again, but she pours the rest of the dressing onto the salad. In my mind the salad is ruined. I am very angry with her. Her mother and I point out to her that she does whatever she wants without regard for others. We tell her that is why people do not want to be around her.

Joe worked with his associations and the dynamics of the dream. He formed a beginning interpretation of this dream. He understood that he has a feminine side that is impulsive and excessive and that he has a motherlike side that is quite condemning of this behavior. What he did not understand from the dream is why the young feminine behaved in such a manner. Therefore, Joe did the following active imagination dialogue: (J is Joe's interactions, his conscious attitude, and W is the woman's response.)

> J: Why do you keep pouring the dressing when I ask you to stop?
> W: Because I just want to. I am so tired of following orders and doing what I am suppose to do.
> All my life I have done what you wanted me to do—follow the rules, be appropriate. I am angry with you
> for pushing me.
> J: Okay, I see. No great harm was done with the salad. It can be fixed.

W: Yea, it was fun just to watch you and my mother get so uptight. It is fun to have the power over you for a change.

J: Okay, here's the problem. If I let you continue to act out this way, you'll do more than just mess up the salad. You'll cause trouble for me in my job or with my wife. So I'd like to see if we could work out some kind of deal where I listen to you more and sometimes express your wishes. In my life now, where have you been trying to express yourself?

W: When are you going to walk in the woods? You talk about it, but you don't do it. Too many things to do— so perfectly.

J: Why are the woods so important to you?

W: It is a place of life and freedom. It is not civilized and proper. I just love it there. The woods are rich with beauty and danger. When you ignore me, I get mad and make a mess. Just walk with me in the woods, then I'll be cooperative. It is not true that I just do whatever I want without regard for others. I just can't stand being treated so poorly by you.

J: Okay, I get it. I don't make time for you. How about we walk in the woods on Friday?

W: I'd like that.

Through this active imagination Joe got a deeper insight into the reason for his rebellious and impulsive side. He was too out of balance by doing the right thing, while ignoring what would feed his soul. His inner woman had to use unruly measures to get his attention so that she could help him get more into balance. He did show up for his walk with his rebellious, inner friend that Friday and has made these walks a regular part of his life. By that, he averted an inner civil war.

Working with these autonomous parts of our psyche is not easy. It takes time, energy, and focus. Eventually it saves us conflict in our outer life, and helps us to live a life more closely connected to our true nature. Jung's description of this process has heartened me:

It is a very difficult and important question, what we call the technique of dealing with the shadow. There is, as a matter of fact, no technique at all, inasmuch as technique means that there is a known and perhaps even prescribable way to deal with a certain difficulty or task. It is rather a dealing comparable to diplomacy or statesmanship. There is, for instance, no particular technique that would help us to reconcile two political parties opposing each other. It can be a question of good will, or diplomatic cunning or civil war or anything. If one can speak of a technique at all, it consists solely in an attitude. First of all, one has to accept and to take seriously into account the existence of the shadow. Secondly, it is necessary to be informed about its qualities and intentions. Thirdly, long and difficult negotiations will be unavoidable. Nobody can know what the final outcome of such negotiations will be. One only knows that through careful collaboration the problem itself becomes changed.... It is rather a result of the conflict one has to suffer. Such conflicts are never solved by a clever trick or by an intelligent invention but by enduring them.[1]

Doing active imagination whether with dream characters or with our projections, is an exercise that brings surprising insights and help for us to live a more conscious life. When we do so, we are making the soul come to life. Over time we will find ourselves more animated and able to live the deepest truths of our lives. We will know ourselves more than ever, and we will realize that a force within us is leading us to a more whole and complete life. As previously stated, by working with our psyche in this way, we are developing our skill in using our Grail King Sword—gaining power and authority in matters of our inner world.

The Story and Commentary

Because of the grief of being separated from his wife Condwiramurs, Parzival leaves Arthur's court as the wedding feast is about to begin. He is riding along the edge of the forest when a pagan knight from the Middle East emerges from the forest. Like Parzival, this knight is also a great warrior. In fact, he has recently led twenty-five armies to Europe. When both warriors see each other, they instinctively react. With spears lowered, they charge one another. At this moment Parzival is reenacting the occasion when Amfortas the Grail King was wounded— a pagan knight from the Middle East emerges from the forest.

An intense battle takes place. It surprises the pagan knight that his first blow does not unseat Parzival. Parzival is aware that this will be the stiffest battle of his life. Both combatants deliver many blows. Splinters fly as spears meet shields; sparks fly as swords meet helmets. Soon both Parzival and the pagan knight are off their horses and battling on foot. It is a desperate struggle. Both men are weakening when the pagan knight calls out the name of his homeland. As he does, he begins to regain his strength. Parzival is down on his knees and begins to think of Condwiramurs and his sons. He shouts the name of his homeland. Just then Condwiramurs' love travels across four kingdoms and reaches Parzival. Now he regains his strength. Parzival rises to his feet and with one mighty blow of his sword strikes the pagan knight on his helmet. However, for the first time since he won his sword from the Red Knight, it shatters. Parzival is defenseless. For the first time in his life he faces defeat and possibly death.

The pagan knight sees the situation and astonishes Parzival by saying, "I cannot kill an unarmed man. Besides, if your sword had not broken, I fear you would have defeated me." The pagan knight invites Parzival to sit with him and rest. Parzival gratefully accepts the pagan knight's invitation. The two men begin to talk, asking each other where they come from and who they are. The pagan knight says that his father comes from Anjou. Parzival in amazement says, "That is my land." At that moment both men discover that they have the same father! The pagan whom Parzival has been fighting, is his brother Feirefiz. Feirefiz wants to see Parzival's face; therefore, he throws his sword away and both men take off their helmets. Parzival sees his black and white brother. They kiss and embrace. As we have seen in the image of the magpie, the black and white now realize that they are connected to each other—they share the same blood. The two brothers have reenacted and corrected the Cain and Abel story; this time a man does not kill his brother. Wolfram gives us a beautiful account of their battle and their reunion:

> The heathen swung his sword aloft, and many of his blows were so dealt that Parzival sank to his knees. One may say that "they" were fighting this way if one wants to speak of them as two, but they are indeed one, for "my brother and I," that is one flesh, just as is a good man and good wife.[2]
> Then neither of them lost any time, each immediately removed his helmet and coif of mail from his head. Parzival found a precious find and the dearest one he ever found. The heathen was recognized at once, for he had the markings of the magpie. With kisses Feirefiz and Parzival concluded their enmity, and friendship beseemed them both better than heart's hatred against one another. Faith and love rendered that battle decision.[3]

The two brothers have a long talk. Feirefiz tells Parzival about his armies, and that he has come to Europe in search of his father. Sadly, he discovers that his father Gahmuret is dead. Both mourn this loss. Parzival then tells his brother about his adventures and about Arthur and his court. Feirefiz has heard of Arthur and would love to meet him. Parzival tells him that Arthur and his court are nearby, and that there is a great wedding feast where there are many beautiful women. Feirefiz wants to go—he has the same appreciation for beautiful women as his father did.

The two brothers ride into Arthur's court. Everyone marvels at Feirefiz. They find him strong and handsome, and his black and white skin fascinates them. Parzival is proud to introduce Feirefiz to his friend Gawain. "He is my father's son." Feirefiz then meets Arthur. It is a happy and wonderful time for Parzival and Feirefiz. The men exchange tales of their adventures, while the women swoon over Feirefiz. The wedding feast is marvelous for all. Parzival wishes that this time would never end, but he has more to experience.

Parzival's wonderful time in Arthur's court is about to be interrupted. A figure riding a mule appears on the horizon. The old mule is tall, and has split nostrils; it is wearing a richly-embroidered harness and bridle. A maiden sits on the mule. She wears a blue cloak and a fancy hat with a peacock feather in it. Her hair is braided and hangs down onto the mule. Her hair is black, thick and about as soft as pig bristles. Today she wears a veil. Her nose resembles that of a dog, while two tusk-like teeth protrude six inches out of her mouth. Her eyebrows are thick, braided, and tied with ribbons to her hair. Her ears are shaped like those of a bear. She carries a whip with a ruby handle in her hand, whose skin is the color of monkey skin. Her fingernails are like lion claws. Here again is Cundrie the messenger from the Grail Castle.

Arthur's court fears that Cundrie's arrival will ruin their wonderful feast. However, much to everyone's surprise Cundrie greets Arthur and the Queen properly. She then turns to Parzival, and with all the courtesy at her command, she falls at his feet and begs for his greeting. Her sincerity so moves Parzival that he loses all his misgivings toward Cundrie. She gets to her feet and takes off her veil, so all can see who she is. To Parzival she says, "Blessed are you, son of Gahmuret! God means to manifest his mercy in you." She greets Feirefiz. Then she tells Parzival that an inscription has appeared on the Grail that states that he is to be Lord of the Grail. She also tells him that his wife Condwiramurs has been named Queen of the Grail. Cundrie tells Parzival that she will lead him back to the Grail Castle where he will greet the suffering King, and with his question will restore Amfortas to health.

Cundrie's message astonishes Parzival. What he had so relentlessly been seeking so many years, now comes to him as grace. He begins to weep tears of joy. Wolfram calls these tears "the fountain springs of the heart." Parzival thanks Cundrie for delivering this wonderful news, and he asks her what he must do. She tells him that he must take a companion with him to the Grail Castle. Parzival can only think of one person to invite—his brother Feirefiz. This is a remarkable moment. Many a baptized person has longed to arrive at the Grail Castle, but now Parzival chooses his heathen brother to be his sacred companion for the healing of the wounded King. Parzival's choice of Feirefiz means that he has made peace with his own shadow. Now he is prepared for the task of healing the wounded King. The three—Parzival, Feirefiz, and Cundrie—take leave of Arthur and his court. The women of the court hate to see Parzival and Feirefiz leave; never have they seen and enjoyed two more handsome men. Cundrie provides safe passage to the Grail Castle for the two brothers.

Meanwhile at the Grail Castle Amfortas has been enduring severe suffering, ever since the day Parzival failed to ask the question. He often wished that he would die, but he is kept alive by the presence of the Grail. Amfortas greets the two brothers joyously, but signs of his suffering are evident on his face. Parzival greets the King and asks where the Grail is. When he is told where it is kept, Parzival turns in that direction, genuflects three times, and prays for help. He then rises to his feet, and with all the compassion and care of an open heart, and with his pagan brother at his side, he addresses the question to the wounded King. "Uncle, what is it that ails you?" In an instant, the King is healed and well again. His skin becomes radiant. Joy returns to the inhabitants of the castle—their sorrow melts away. The Waste Land is healed! All declare Parzival the Lord of the Grail Castle.

This moment is clearly the climax of the story—the healing of the Grail King and the healing of the Waste Land. The turning point that makes the healing of the wounded King possible is Parzival's meeting and making peace with Feirefiz. In the opening paragraph of the story, Wolfram introduced us to the idea that we are like the magpie—both black and white. However, our religious and social training has taught us to strive to be only white. Parzival has achieved union with his dark brother. Whoever wishes to heal the wounded King within himself must first make peace with his own dark, pagan self—his shadow. He must come to accept and love in himself all that seems unworthy of the Grail. In this culture we are socialized to deny and to be ashamed of this essential part of our nature. Like Parzival, at first we are hostile toward our shadow self. We do not recognize it as our dark brother. We see it as a stranger and a threat. This battle with Feirefiz was the stiffest for Parzival, and it is for us. If we are hostile toward our brother, inner or outer, we cannot draw near the Grail. From the perspective of the inner life, Parzival's journey shows the importance of working with our shadow material, whether in dreams or in our projections. If we can accept in ourselves what we have been taught is unacceptable, then we can accept those qualities in others. When we reject shadow qualities in ourselves, we will reject other people when we see those same qualities in them. Therefore, our lives will have many unnecessary conflicts. When a person embraces his previously rejected shadow, he releases an enormous amount of healing and creative energy. Without the release of this great energy that our shadow contains, we cannot heal our own wounded King.

Parzival, the new Grail King, has several more matters to which he must attend. Amfortas has sent Sigune's father, a Grail Knight, to Parzival's land to lead Condwiramurs and their two sons to the Grail Land. Condwiramurs and her sons have encamped on the same meadow where years before the three drops of blood had entranced Parzival. No longer is there a fantasy; the real person Condwiramurs is there now. Parzival leaves the Grail Castle to meet his wife and sons, and to accompany them back to the Castle.

On his way Parzival stops at the cave of the hermit Trevrizent, who rejoices at the news that his brother Amfortas is healed. He admits to Parzival that he was wrong, when he told him that no one could return to the Grail Castle a second time. He tells Parzival that by his persistence and tenacity he has changed the laws of God. The law that a person can only come to the Grail once apparently was a man-made law that was ascribed to God. Parzival's instinct to continue searching for the Grail, despite the admonition from Trevrizent, shows that the inner laws of the heart supercede man-made religious laws. Parzival has found his own inner authority; he now listens to the god within. Parzival no longer wears the Fool's Clothing; he has developed his own inner knowing and lives from that truth.

In the morning, after a tender parting from Trevrizent, Parzival rides to the tent where Condwiramurs and his sons are staying. They rejoice at their reunion; their lengthy separation has been difficult for all. Parzival is reunited with the love of his life. This time he sees the real human being Condwiramurs, and not the illusion in the snow.

Parzival then leads his wife and children to the Grail Castle. On the way they come to the hermitage of Sigune. They find her slumped in a kneeling position at the grave of her dead knight. She too is dead. Parzival gives her a proper burial. When he opens the tomb of Sigune's dead knight, he finds that his body is not decayed. Parzival places Sigune in the grave with her love. Throughout the story Sigune mirrors Parzival's relationship to his own soul. For all this time she is separated from her beloved. Now they are united; Sigune finally rests with her beloved in the eternal realm. This image is symbolical of Parzival finally coming to rest with his own soul. Psychologically, he has made the reality of the Self conscious in his body and in his action. Parzival is experiencing the inner marriage — the union of the feminine and the masculine. This union literally makes a soul live. When one realizes such a union, he experiences the numinous in everyday life; he is present to the creative, eternal now. Parzival is consciously living the process of individuation.

Parzival brings his family to the Grail Castle, and proudly introduces Condwiramurs to Feirefiz and then to Amfortas. They are all led back into the Great Hall where the Grail Ceremony takes place. This time Parzival and Condwiramurs sit in the front of the hall, and the bloody spear that had signified Amfortas' wound is no longer present. Into the hall the twenty-five maidens process with Repanse de Schoye carrying the Grail on the green pillow. The Grail provides everyone what she or he desires to eat.

Feirefiz sees Repanse de Schoye, and falls hopelessly in love with her. Never before had he suffered such deep love. Feirefiz can see the Grail Maiden clearly but he is unable to see the Grail. Amfortas is the first to notice that Feirefiz cannot see the Grail, only the woman who carries it. Titurel the first Grail King says that Feirefiz must be baptized before he can see the Grail. The love-struck Feirefiz asks what that means and what he has to do. They tell him that he has to believe in God. He asks if it is the same God in whom Repanse de Schoye believes. The answer is "Yes." That is good enough for Feirefiz, so they baptize him. However, this baptism is not the ordinary church baptism; Feirefiz is baptized with water from the Grail. When they tip the Grail, the water flows out. When Feirefiz is baptized with Grail water, he can see the Grail.

Wolfram tells us that Feirefiz and Repanse de Schoye marry, and in time, they will travel to India where they have a son. Parzival and Condwiramurs continue to live as King and Queen of the Grail Castle.

What does it mean psychologically that Parzival becomes the King of the Grail Castle? The King is the symbol of wholeness and the achievement of union with the Self. From this point of view, the King is one who has united the opposites of the psyche within himself. He has unified the energy and the freedom of youth with the wisdom and experience of age. The masculine and the feminine have become united within him—just as Sigune has become one with her beloved. Union of the masculine and feminine is the union of the conscious and the unconscious and the union of spirit and matter. When this happens the Waste Land is redeemed, that is, creativity and life force flow again. Life is renewed with added meaning, values, and purpose.

When one reaches this state, a peaceful and harmonious kingdom is created within the person and with his relationship to others and to the world. However, this peaceful kingdom is not an idealistic, naive life. The true King of the Grail knows his own shadow. He understands its power, and his ability to do good or harm. He also understands the shadow in others, and their ability to do good or harm. It is with this knowledge that he can make a realistic peace within himself and with others. To put this another way, the Grail King has made the connection with the reality of the Self, and can live a life from that perspective. When Parzival becomes the Grail King, he is realizing individuation. This action transforms the sadness and sorrow that existed in the kingdom ever since the day Amfortas killed the pagan knight. True wholeness and authentic living are restored.

It is also important to note that not only is Parzival named the King of the Grail, but that Condwiramurs is also named Queen of the Grail. In the previous era, Amfortas ruled without a wife—the feminine was missing. When the Grail ceremony takes place, Parzival and Condwiramurs sit at the front of the Grail Hall presiding over the ceremony. The myth of Parzival is ushering in a new era that emphasizes the importance of the feminine. We also see this emphasis of the feminine in the Gawain segment of the story when he frees the four queens and the four hundred maidens. In his Grail legend Wolfram is saying that we cannot achieve wholeness unless we bring the feminine into her rightful place within our psyche, and therefore, within our world. When this union with our inner feminine occurs, a new essence of love infuses our inner King and radiates through our whole being. Wolfram gives us a wonderful image for the union of the masculine and the feminine when he has Trevrizent tell Parzival about the Grail and its annual renewal. Trevrizent reports that every Good Friday a dove comes from heaven and places a white host on the Grail. This action renews the Grail's vitality for the year. In other words, when the masculine spirit brings the bread from heaven and when the feminine container of the Grail opens to receive it, new life is created. Spring is the symbol of the creative impulse that results from this union of the masculine and the feminine. During this season the earth is revitalized with new life: grass becomes green again, leaves reappear, days become longer, birds sing their mating songs as they build their nests for their young, and joy fills the air with the sights, sounds, and smells of renewal. The same process occurs in each person's being when the masculine and the feminine are united. Life is renewed and creative energy is released. The old ways are replaced with possibilities.

The idea of giving the feminine its rightful place in life was a radical idea for the listeners of the thirteenth century, and it is a radical idea in many quarters today. Nowadays mocking the idea of developing one's feminine side is fashionable, since we often repress and oppress that which we fear. It is easy to pay lip-service to the feminine without doing the hard work of opening to this dimension of the psyche. To open to the reality of the feminine within one's psyche, and to make it an equal life partner is a very difficult, although necessary task. Parzival and Gawain had to overcome many obstacles, before they could achieve an integration of the feminine and so do we. The collective forces that ignore and repress this feminine reality and the inner world are centuries old and very compelling. It takes a major commitment, and a warrior's mentality to make the feminine life force a real and equal partner in our life. Freeing and partnering with the feminine is a major task to accomplish to reach our own Grail. It is also one of the most important psychological tasks of our times.

So ends the tale of Parzival and his journey from innocence, through a great period of doubt, to reach his destiny of soulfulness. May our journey have so rich an outcome.

The Questions

1. Projection is the unconscious mechanism by which I see my unaccepted qualities reflected back to me through another person.

   Think about someone to whom you have a strong aversion. What qualities do you not like? Can you see where those qualities are operating in your life? What if you could accept this part of yourself? Write about this.

   Think about someone whom you greatly admire. What are the qualities that are so appealing to you? Can you see how those qualities could be a part of your personality? What if you could accept this part of yourself? Write about this.

2. Take an honest look at your wound: the area in you where you suffer and find meaninglessness. Look at yourself in this place and with compassion ask yourself: "What is really troubling me?" Write about this.

3. Take a character or a symbol from one of your dreams and do active imagination with it.

   -Invite the image.

   -Dialogue with it—write the dialogue and interactions.

   -Bring your human values to the dialogue.

   -Do a ritual to honor the event.

4. What have you done to unite the masculine with the feminine parts of your personality? What do you still need to do to accomplish this task?

5. In response to finishing the Parzival myth:

   -What part of the story touched you?

   -Where could you relate to his journey?

   -What did you learn about yourself through this story?

   -With what questions does the story leave you?

Chapter Ten

Reflections
Inner Life

This book is a guide for the man who wants to pursue an inner life in a serious and meaningful way. It has been a joy for me to watch men begin to find life-giving energy in their inner world—a world they had previously discounted or did not even know existed. What we all discover very quickly is that to have an active and meaningful relationship to our inner world takes work, just as it takes work to create a meaningful outer life. One day in one of my men's groups, a fellow was discussing his recent dream, and he began to see the deeper meaning in it. This was exciting for him. However, when he realized that he would have to do more work, including active imagination, his face took on a serious look. He said, "Boy, this is a lot of work." Yes, it is, and doing it alone is really hard. When I run up against my resistence to spending the time to work on my inner life, I think of the Fram oil filter commercial. In the ad the mechanic tells the man who needs an engine overhaul how much cheaper it is to change the oil and filter regularly. "But it is up to you," he says. "Pay me now or pay me later." I think this is the attitude of the unconscious. In the end spending time regularly to develop a meaningful relationship with my inner world is more productive and efficient. If I do so, I will prevent myself from having to face the same issues in my relationships in my outer life. Remember Jung said that what we do not deal with consciously comes to us as fate. It takes discipline and commitment to change the oil regularly, but over time, it is easier than having to do an engine overhaul, that is to repair damage in one's life because of years of neglect.

As men we have been socialized away from the inner world—we are told that is for women or children. Since the resistence to this work is great, I suggest that men find either a trusted guide or group to help them along the way. It is a blessing to find even one other man who is willing to share, support, challenge, and to be challenged in this way. I have seen men go through several stages before they can see the need to focus on their inner life. One man said, "My wife dragged me into all this. At first I resisted her, then I did it for her, but now I am doing it for myself." That man is beginning to find emotional freedom.

Men experience a deep sense of satisfaction, when they discover that they can tap into a deep well of creative energy within themselves. When they do so, their faces relax, brighten, and a childlike pleasure emanates from them. I have had the honor recently of sitting around a table with twelve men as they shared their dreams and active imagination work. While they did so, the burdens of their work life and the struggles of their relationships faded. I witnessed these men as their spirits became animated when they connected with their feminine source. This experience reminded me of what Sigune told Parzival— that there is a well that contains water from the Source, and that this water can renew the sword of the Grail King. The inner life is the well. These men are learning to contact the waters from that well, and they are gaining skill and proficiency in using their second sword, their inner authority and empowerment. My experience is that men are hungry for the life within. However, they need someone to show them the way to this world, and they want other men who will go there with them to provide a safe and nonjudgmental container for this experience.

When a person begins to form a relationship with his inner world, he will experience an unmistakable truth: a reality, different from his conscious awareness, lives within him. This other reality is observing his life through his dreams, and it is commenting on his life—challenging, guiding, and supporting him. Many of us find comfort and hope in this truth. In the introduction of this book, we met Sigune the grieving, human soul who observes, confronts, and supports Parzival. She is his invisible companion who appears at key moments of his journey to teach, to give guidance, and to show him his relationship to his soul. One group member who studied the Parzival tale reported a powerful dream that spoke of this inner observer. When he was in his early teens, he dreamed that he and his family were at his grave, and they were all weeping for him. Now, thirty-five years later he realizes the importance of that dream. Because of the emotional difficulties of his mother, this man learned to deny his own needs and his own life path. He developed a behavioral style that he hoped would please his mother, so that he would not be an additional burden to her. He now realizes that his dream from his teenage years was an experience of his own Sigune. Although he did not realize it at the time, he was dead to his authentic self and had become a soulless boy for his family. However, he also recognized that something within him was grieving for him and for his loss of soul connection. Some part within him kept vigil all these years, as he made his way out of his family-prescribed role and into a solid and meaningful reunion with his own true nature. This was a powerful dream and an inspiring story of a man who became lost, but with great persistence found his way back to himself. It is a deep comfort for him to know that, just as Sigune wept for Parzival, a part of his psyche grieved for him and waited for his return.

I offer one final observation about the inner life. Many men put an enormous amount of weight and meaning on their sexual lives. For many of us, it is one of the only times we feel alive, safe, or comforted. However, if our partner begins to have a different (and it is usually less) interest in making love than we do, we become troubled, because we feel cut off from a major part of life. It is then easy to resort to anger or power games, as Clamidé did, to feel connected, loved, and worthwhile again. Of course, this tactic rarely works and most men then feel powerless. At these times, when you feel so powerless to change the situation, you can do one thing that will make a difference. Begin to form a relationship with your own inner woman. Ask yourself what you are feeling under your anger, and share that with your partner—without expectations that the other will change. Share it because you want to be emotionally honest and relational. The experience will change you forever. It has been my experience that if a man can really focus on his inner life during times of disconnection, it often has a positive effect on his relationship with his partner. He creates more space for the two of them to find new territory in which to reconnect.

I hope that you have been encouraged by the examples of ordinary men, who are beginning to value their inner life and who are making it a priority. If you are curious about whether you could develop a similar relationship with your inner world, place a pen and paper next to your bed tonight. Ask your unconscious to speak to you about your deepest and most authentic self, and ask it to show you how you might bring that self into being. If you do so, you will embark on a marvelous journey, and you will be investing in a great treasure—your soul.

The Story and Commentary

I was drawn to Wolfram's Grail legend, because it spoke to me about many experiences that I have had in my life. That is the power of a myth. Myths give us a container and a road map in which we can see our own story. Such myths are very important in our modern times, because religious organizations no longer hold significance for many people. When traditional religious systems no longer provide meaning for us, then we must find a myth that speaks to us, and gives us a context in which we can see our lives as part of a larger reality. We need a myth that gives us hope and direction, when we are experiencing our period(s) of doubt. Since Wolfram's tale spoke to me, I began to tell the Parzival story to other men. I have been quite moved to see men talk to each other about this myth, and where they could see themselves in the story. Almost every man who has heard this story can see his Fool's Clothing. How freeing it is for men to talk about this universal tendency to be taken care of, to have an image to help them see this dynamic in their lives, and to find guidance in the tale that helps them address this deep-seated attitude. Most men talk with tenderness about the men who have mentored them over the years. As they do, their own desire to be a mentor for other men emerges. The spirit of Gurnemanz and Trevrizent continues to live in the hearts of men who hear this story. The idea of one's personal wound and one's own Waste Land within is a difficult notion for some men to acknowledge. However, hearing other men struggle to articulate how the wounded Grail King lives in them and how it creates the experience of their own Waste Land, often encourages a man to risk looking at and admitting the painful reality of his wounding. Acknowledging our common struggles is comforting and encouraging for most men.

Each time I tell this story, I am moved by the scene where Parzival and Feirefiz recognize each other as brothers and not as enemies. I believe this scene holds the essential wisdom of Wolfram's Grail legend. We live in a world of opposites and opposition. People are categorized by their adversaries as liberal or conservative, Christian or non-Christian, Christian or the wrong kind of Christian, black or white, aggressive woman or dominating man, or many other divisive stereotypes. According to the Parzival story, this tendency to dehumanize our fellow human beings by placing them in camps that seem foreign to us is one manifestation of the Waste Land. Until Parzival recognized as his brother, the Moslem knight who did not know Christ, he was not able to return to the Grail and end his time of self-alienation. Wolfram's story emphasizes the point that Carl Jung made six hundred years later: if a person wants to make a positive contribution to solving the social ills of his time, he must learn to recognize and embrace all within himself that seems foreign to his ego-identity. He must learn to embrace his shadow, the dark brother or sister within. Owning one's shadow is a critical task on which the well-being of our planet depends. Whenever a person feels overwhelmed by the magnitude of our social ills, and is tempted to say that there is nothing that he can do, he can work on owning his shadow and on accepting his dark brother. In our current time, if we would be guided to face and accept our inner terrorist while our nation fights the "war on terrorism," we would be doing our part in that struggle. When a person does this work, it changes the way he relates to other people, especially strangers, and it opens new possibilities for his involvement in social justice and other needs of his society.

In our Grail story the question that heals the wounded King is extremely significant. Parzival asks, "What ails you?" In other versions of the Grail legend the healing question is, "Whom does the Grail serve?" Wolfram's tale is the only one that focuses the healing question on the King's ailment. Why is the wound so important to Wolfram? Why does compassionately asking about the wound bring the longed-for healing? In my own life and in the lives of those I counsel, I have witnessed the important truth that Wolfram's story highlights: the wound is the opening to the Divine. It is precisely in our wounding that God can reach us. When we experience the effects of our wounding, we often feel powerless to overcome our intense pain. Then we look back over our life and discover that our defenses against this pain have lead us into self-defeating and self-sabotaging behavior. We see a life that we can never redo—a startling realization. At this moment of realization, we have the opportunity to reach out beyond our self, as Parzival does, for the succor, guidance, and love to take us through our wound to an experience of transformation.

Wolfram's healing question focuses on the Grail King's wound because it is the way to the Divine. A woman once told me a story that illustrates this point. In her thirties she began an inner journey. She discovered not only her unconscious childhood wounding, but a deep connection to the spiritual realm. One day she told her spiritual advisor that one of her deepest regrets was that she did not have her new awareness earlier, when her children were very young. She feared that she had wounded them through her own lack of consciousness. Her advisor told her that her love and care for her children would overcome much of the pain that she caused them. However, the most comforting realization that he gave her was that it would be precisely in the areas that she had failed her children that they would one day come to feet of the Divine.

Wolfram's story of Parzival tells us to compassionately ask ourselves, "What ails me, at the soul level?" That question, honestly asked, will heal our wounded Grail King and lead us to the Divine. To experience the Grail is to experience the god within. It is to know this truth in one's bones: "I am a spirit in a body and I am connected to the world of the Infinite." The Grail experience is a feminine portal through the world of the opposites into the world of unity, wholeness, and a new essence of love. Ultimately, this is the destiny of every human soul. As C. G. Jung wrote:

> The decisive question for man is: Is he related to something infinite or not? That is the telling question of his life. Only if we know that thing which truly matters is the infinite, can we avoid fixing our interests upon futilities and upon all kinds of goals which are not of real importance...If we understand and feel that here in this life we already have a link with the infinite, desires and attitudes change. In the final analysis, we count for something only because of the essential we embody, and if we do not embody that, life is wasted. In our relationships to other men, too, the critical question is whether an element of boundlessness is expressed in that relationship. The feeling for the infinite, however, can be attained only if we are bound to the utmost.[1]

In the introduction of this book, we heard the story of the Grail appearing veiled to the Knights of the Round Table. After the Grail disappeared, Gawain encouraged each knight to seek the Grail unveiled—an invitation for each man to discover his own unique path to the Grail. The image of the unveiled Grail holds a great significance for us. When the Grail is veiled, the seeker cannot see its full power and vibrancy. When veiled the Grail may be honored and valued, however, it is unable to communicate its full spiritual power because the collective, religious institutions are themselves split and wounded. Therefore, they are unable to reveal the full spiritual message of Grail; it remains veiled. However, the experience of the Grail unveiled can occur when the split between the spiritual and the instinctual in the individual is healed. Only when Parzival experiences the depth of his own suffering during his period of doubt and finally makes peace with his shadow brother, his instinctual nature, could he experience the full vitality of the Grail. Only then could he heal the wounded King. The same is true for our journey. We must first come to accept and integrate our instinctual, uncivilized nature in order to open our awareness to the universal connection of all life—our highest spiritual insight. In order for a person to live from this awesome reality, he must develop a strong ego personality to contain and hold the reality of the god alive within himself. To know this truth in one's bones is to experience the Grail unveiled. Occasionally a person will attempt to open to these deep spiritual truths without first integrating his instinctual animal nature. Doing so is not wise, because his ability to contain his full self is not yet developed and he will be unable to integrate the deeper spiritual truths into his life. He can easily become overwhelmed and disoriented by the experience. When a person realizes that all that the cultural, religious institutions has been carrying for him now live within him, he may become disoriented by this radical change of perspective. It takes time to integrate our instinctual and shadow self. We must face the truth that all that seemed unworthy of the spiritual life lives within us. We must embrace all of our nature so that we can accept and contain our full spiritual identity and potential. This experience is the Grail unveiled.

Wolfram ends the Parzival tale by telling the reader that he has told the tale accurately as he received it from his source. He ends with this postscript:

> His children and his high race I have rightly named for you, Parzival's I mean, whom I brought to the place which, in spite of everything, his blessedness had destined for him. A life so concluded that God is not robbed of the soul through fault of the body, and which can obtain the world's favor with dignity, *that* is a worthy work.[2]

I have always been struck by that last sentence about God not being robbed of the soul through fault of the body. The teaching of the time was that what robbed God of a soul was the body—the world of instincts, the passions, the earthy, the feminine, the unconscious, nature, and the world of matter. Therefore, that instruction stressed that the world of the body needed to be suppressed and overcome. Ever since Eve was blamed for the Fall, the body and the world it represents have been suspect. This is still the teaching in many quarters today. Through the story of Parzival, Wolfram is presenting a radically different philosophy—what robs God of a soul is not the fault of the body, but rather the denying, rejecting, and attempting to kill all that the body represents. This was Amfortas' great mistake—killing the pagan knight. This action left him impotent; it leaves us spiritually impotent—soulless.

To live soulfully on this earth means to accept, embrace, and come to terms with all that is in me. This is what Parzival did. Sigune first told Parzival his true name and what it means: "one who pierces the valley" and "right through the middle." Parzival pierces the valley of his nature by not identifying with either side, but by living in the middle. When he does so, he sees on the right side the masculine mountain of spirit, intellect, the rational, ideals, and spiritual values, and on the left side, he sees the feminine mountain of matter, emotions, instincts, the body, the value of being relational, and the unconscious. Through his life journey he learned to hold both realities and integrate them into his life. Psychologically, this means that Parzival experienced the process of individuation. He came to live an authentic life.

When a person has the courage to become a Parzival, he or she is allowed to breathe fully into and live from all the energies that make him or her human. By that, God is not robbed of a soul—an authentic soul is made. Now that *is* a worthy work for any man or woman.

Whatever struck you in this tale says something about you and the mystery of life that is unfolding through you. Continue to examine that section of the story. Ask yourself what it reveals about you. What are you to learn about yourself through this part of the tale? Let Parzival's journey be a guide for you as you explore the mystery of your own life. May your journey continue until you reach the full embodiment of your soul—your experience of the Grail.

Jesus said:
If those who guide your Being say to you:
"Behold the Kingdom is in the heaven,"
then the birds of the sky will precede you;
if they say to you: "It is in the sea."
then the fish will precede you.
But the Kingdom is in your center
and is about you.
When you know your Self
then you will be known,

and you will be aware that you are
the sons (and daughters) of the Living Father.
But if you do not know yourselves
then you live in poverty,
and you are the poverty.
(Gnostic Gospel of Thomas, logion 3)

Cast of Characters

Amfortas	The wounded Grail King.
Arthur	King of the Round Table.
Belacane	African queen; wife of Gahmuret and mother of Feirefiz.
Clamidé	Unwelcome suitor of Condwiramurs; defeated by Parzival.
Clinschor	King of the Castle of Wonders. Symbol of patriarchy.
Condwiramurs	Parzival's wife. Her name means "channel of love."
Cundrie	Uncomely messenger from the Grail Castle.
Cunneware	A lady in Arthur's court whose laugh designated young Parzival as the most worthy knight to come to the court.
Feirefiz	Black and white brother of Parzival. Son of Gahmuret and Belacane.
Gahmuret	Father of Parzival and Feirefiz. Husband to Herzeloyde and Belacane.
Gawain	Knight of Arthur's court. Parzival's dear friend. Frees the Castle of Wonders and marries Orgeluse.
Gramoflanz	Guardian of the wreath tree. Scheduled to battle Gawain. Marries Gawain's sister.
Ginover	Wife of Arthur
Gurnemanz	Old knight who teaches Parzival knightly combat skills and the ethics of knighthood.
Herzeloyde	Mother of Parzival and wife of Gahmuret.
Jeshute	Wife of Orilus. Woman in the tent.
Keie	Ill-tempered Knight of Arthur's court. Struck Cunneware and the dwarf. Eventually defeated by Parzival.
Laize	Daughter of Gurnemanz. Parzival's first love.
Orgeluse	Seducer of Amfortas. Becomes the wife of Gawain.
Orilus	Knight who stole Parzival's land and killed Sigune's beloved. Husband of Jeshute. Defeated by Parzival.

Parzival   Son of Gahmuret and Herzeloyde. Hero of the tale.

Red Knight   Ither. A great knight. Killed by young Parzival for his armor.

Repanse de Schoye Grail maiden. Carries Grail during the ceremony. Marries Feirefiz.

Sigune   Parzival's cousin who holds her dead knight. Symbolic of Parzival's relationship to his own soul.

Titurel   The first Grail King. Parzival's great-grandfather.

Trevrizent   Brother of Amfortas. Parzival's spiritual teacher.

Bibliography

Campbell, Joseph.   *Myths to Live By*. New York: Viking Press, 1972.
                    The Power of Myth. New York: Doubleday, 1988.
                    Transformations of Myth Through Time. (audio-tape series) St. Paul, MN: Highbridge   Productions, 1990.
Cain, Sarah C.   *The Coloring Book*.
Dunn, Claire.   *Carl Jung: Wounded Healer of the Soul*. New York: Parabola Books, 2000.
Johnson, Robert A. *The Fisher King and the Handless Maiden*. New York: Harper Collins. 1993.
                   He. King of Prussia, Pa: Religious Publishing Co. 1974.
                   Inner Work. New York: Harper and Row. 1986.
                   Lying with the Heavenly Woman. New York: HarperCollins, 1994.
Jung, C.G.   *The Collected Works* (Bollingen Series XX). 20 vols. Trans.
                   R.F.C. Hull Ed. H. Read, M. Fordham, G. Adler, Wm. McGuire. Princeton: Princeton University Press, 1953-1979.
                   Memories, Dreams, Reflections. Recorded and edited by Aniela Jaffé. New York: Vintage Books. 1989
McGregor-Ross, H, *The Gospel of Thomas*. Great Britain: Element Books, 1987.
Sanford, John A.   *King Saul, The Tragic Hero*. New York: Paulist Press.1985.
Stein, Johannes W *The Ninth Century*. London: Temple Lodge Press, 1988.
Von Eschenbach,   *Parzival*. Trans. H.M. Mustard and C.E. Passage.
Wolfram   New York: Vintage Books, 1961.
Woodman, Marion *The Ravaged Bridegroom*. Toronto: Inner City Books, 1990.

Endnotes

Book Cover
Picture of Montsegur courtesy of Peggy Leutelle.

Preface
1. For a wonderful discussion of this topic see Marion Woodman. *The Ravaged Bridegroom*.

Introduction
1. Robert Bly, Minnesota Men's Conference, 1989.
2. Joseph Campbell. *Myths to Live By*.
3. Walter Stein. *The Ninth Century*.

Chapter One
1. Wolfram von Eschenbach, *Parzival*. translated by Helen M. Mustard and Charles E. Passage. p.3.
2. Ibid. Pp. 57-58.
3. Ibid. p. 61.

Chapter Two
1. Walter Stein. *The Ninth Century*.
2. Wolfram p. 67.
3. Ibid p. 72.
4. Marion Woodman. The Ravaged Bridegroom, p 31.
5. For further discussion see Robert Johnson. *He*.

Chapter Three
1. Robert Johnson. *He*. Pp. 26-28.
2. Wolfram, p. 90.

Chapter Four
1. C.G. Jung, "Psychology and Religion," CW 11, par 140.
2. For an in depth discussion of the anima and the feeling function read

Robert Johnson *Lying with the Heavenly Woman* and *The Fisher King and the Handless Maiden*.

3. John Sanford. King Saul, The Tragic Hero.

4. Wolfram, p. 110.

5. Joseph Campbell. *Myths to Live By*.

Chapter Five

1. For a full and rich discussion of this method read *Inner Work* by Robert Johnson.

2. Wolfram p.129.

3. Ibid. p.134.

Chapter Six

1. Wolfram p. 170.

2. Ibid. Pp. 170-171.

Chapter Seven

1. Ibid. p. 177.

2. Ibid. p. 178.

3. C.G. Jung, *Psychology and Religion*, CW 1, par 522.

Chapter Eight

1. Stein, Walter J. *The Ninth Century. World History in Light of the Holy Grail*. Pp. 223-229. I am grateful to Mr. Stein for his thoughts about the Bed of Wonders.

Chapter Nine

1. Jung. *Collected Letters*, Vol. 1 page 234.

2. Wolfram, p. 386.

3. Ibid. p 390.

Chapter Ten

1. *Carl Jung: Wounded Healer of the Soul*. Page 167.

2. Wolfram, Pp. 430-431.

End

760788

Made in the USA